Documents and Debates
Louis XIV and France

Documents and Debates
General Editor: John Wroughton M.A., F.R.Hist.S.

Louis XIV and France

Victor Mallia-Milanes M.A., Ph.D., F.R.Hist.S.

Acting-Head, History, The New Lyceum (Arts), Malta

MACMILLAN

First published 1986

Published by
MACMILLAN EDUCATION LTD
Houndmills, Basingstoke, Hampshire RG21 2XS
and London
Companies and representatives
throughout the world

Typeset by Wessex Typesetters
(Division of The Eastern Press Ltd)
Frome, Somerset

Printed in Hong Kong

British Library Cataloguing in Publication Data
Mallia-Milanes, Victor
Louis XIV and France—(Documents and debates)
1. France—History—Louis XIV, 1643–1715
I. Title   II. Series
944'.033   DC125
ISBN 0–333–39145–4

For Mary, Keith, Victoria, Kenneth

Contents

General Editor's Preface

This book forms part of a series entitled *Documents and Debates*, which is aimed primarily at sixth formers. The earlier volumes in the series each covered approximately one century of history, using material both from original documents and from modern historians. The more recent volumes, however, are designed in response to the changing trends in history examinations at 18 plus, most of which now demand the study of documentary sources and the testing of historical skills. Each volume therefore concentrates on a particular topic within a narrower span of time. It consists of eight sections, each dealing with a major theme in depth, illustrated by extracts drawn from primary sources. The series intends partly to provide experience for those pupils who are required to answer questions on documentary material at A-level, and partly to provide pupils of all abilities with a digestible and interesting collection of source material, which will extend the normal textbook approach.

This book is designed essentially for the pupil's own personal use. The author's introduction will put the period as a whole into perspective, highlighting the central issues, main controversies, available source material and recent developments. Although it is clearly not our intention to replace the traditional textbook, each section will carry its own brief introduction, which will set the documents into context. A wide variety of source material has been used in order to give the pupils the maximum amount of experience – letters, speeches, newspapers, memoirs, diaries, official papers, Acts of Parliament, Minute Books, accounts, local documents, family papers, etc. The questions vary in difficulty, but aim throughout to compel the pupil to think in depth by the use of unfamiliar material. Historical knowledge and understanding will be tested, as well as basic comprehension. Pupils will also be encouraged by the questions to assess the reliability of evidence, to recognise bias and emotional prejudice, to reconcile conflicting accounts and to extract the essential from the irrelevant. Some questions, *marked with an asterisk*, require knowledge outside the immediate extract and are intended for further research or discussion, based on the pupil's general knowledge of the period. Finally, we hope that students using this material will learn something of the nature of historical inquiry and the role of the historian.

John Wroughton

Acknowledgements

The author and publishers wish to thank the following who have kindly given permission for the use of copyright material:

Banco di Roma for an extract from 'Silk Manufacturing in France and Italy in the XVIIth Century', *Journal of European Economic History*, X (Spring 1981); Professor J. Lough (ed.) and Cambridge University Press for extracts from *John Locke's Travels in France 1675–1679* (1953); Professor D. G. Charlton (ed.) and Methuen & Company Ltd for extracts from *France, A Companion to French Studies*, 2nd edn (1979); J. M. Dent & Sons Ltd for extracts from *The Age of Louis XIV* by Voltaire, trans. M. P. Pollack (Everyman's Library series) (1926); Professor R. M. Hatton for an extract from *Louis XIV and Absolutism*; William Heinemann Ltd for extracts from *The Fables of La Fontaine*, trans. Edward Marsh (1952); The Controller of Her Majesty's Stationery Office for extracts from *Calendar of State Papers* (Venetian), ed. A. B. Hinds (1937); Johns Hopkins University Press for an extract from 'Colbert and the Commerce of Bordeaux' by F. C. Lane, in *Venice and History: The Collected Papers of Frederic C. Lane* (1966); Dr H. G. Judge for extracts from *Louis XIV* (Problems and Perspectives in History series) by Longman Group Ltd (1965); W. W. Norton & Company Inc. and Victor Gollancz Ltd for extracts from *Louis XIV* by J. B. Wolf (1968); Oxford University Press for extracts from *The Diary of John Evelyn*, ed. E. S. de Beer (1959), and from *Early Modern France 1560–1715* by R. Briggs (1977); Prentice-Hall, Inc. for extracts from *Louis XIV* ed. John C. Rule, Copyright © 1974; O. and P. Ranum (eds) and Macmillan Ltd for extracts from *The Century of Louis XIV* (1972); Bell & Hyman Ltd for an extract from *Seventeenth Century France* by G. R. R. Treasure (1966); Dr Leonard Tancock for extracts from his translation of *La Rochefoucauld: Maxims* (Penguin Classics) (reprint 1984); University of Chicago Press for extracts from *The Institutions of France under the Absolute Monarchy 1598–1789* by R. Mousnier, trans. A. Goldhammer (1984); Weidenfeld & Nicholson Ltd for extracts from *The Ancien Régime: French Society 1600–1750* by P. Goubert, trans. S. Cox (1973); Routledge & Kegan Paul Ltd for an extract from *Crisis in Europe 1560–1660*, ed. T. Aston, 5th impression (1975).

Every effort has been made to trace all the copyright holders but if any have been inadvertently overlooked the publishers will be pleased to make the necessary arrangement at the first opportunity.

The cover illustration shows a marble bust of Louis XIV by Gian Lorenzo Bernini. Reproduced by permission of the Mansell Collection.

Louis XIV and France

The year 1680 marked a decisive turning point in French history. 'Most of the events that altered the course of Louis XIV's reign' and the 'destiny of France', says Erlanger, were to occur within 'less than a decade'. It was a turning point for the worse. That year the Council of Paris conferred on Louis XIV the title of *Great*, with all 'due solemnity' and 'excessive adulation'. The king, says Voltaire, 'was at this time at the height of his greatness'. The earlier part of the reign had witnessed his finest and most glittering moments of power and prosperity at home and the aggrandisement of France through military achievements abroad.

On the death of Mazarin in 1661, Louis XIV decided to concentrate power in his own hands and be his own first minister. He would thus be in a position, explains Mousnier, to understand 'the totality of affairs'. For 'maximum efficiency' he charged himself with the burdens of the state and its government. His was the *métier* of the *roi-bureaucrate*. He knew well its implications and lived up to its exacting demands amid courtly pleasures and imposing royal grandeur. After the bitter experience of the Frondes, absolutism was a necessary political expedient and a national desire. The nobles were reduced to mere adulators, complacently absorbed by the ceremonial trappings of courtly life. Ministers were chosen from the 'vile bourgeois' class. 'All eyes were fastened' upon Louis 'alone'. In theory his royal will was divine; in practice it was supreme law. He was every inch a king – *Nec Paribus Impar*.

If the final decisions of the state during Louis XIV's highly centralised administration were incontestably his, one should not, however, overlook his dependence upon the views of the team of 'giant' ministers around him. These were the 'trained élite, capable of carrying the state almost irrespective of the nature or abilities of the government'. The extent of their influence in shaping royal policy – indeed, his very 'notion of glory' – must have been considerable. How truly *his* were the grandiose designs which his government put so effectively into operation? Was the image he and his men created of a secret sovereignty, more powerful and majestic than that of any other monarch in seventeenth-century Europe, a true image of the king? Or was it so awe-inspiring that it enthralled not only Louis' contemporaries and later historians but even its originators to the extent of letting themselves be captivated by the very idea turned into reality?

It was to the work of the loyal and intransigent Jean-Baptiste Colbert that France owed most of its material prosperity and economic revival during these years. French finances were improved and the economic health of the kingdom regained a new strength. Motivated by a genuine desire to meet the ever increasing expenditure of the crown, Colbert set to work indefatigably on a wide programme of reform and reorganisation. He reformed the system of taxation, encouraged industrial growth and development, promoted commercial and colonial expansion and rebuilt the navy 'beyond the hopes of the French and the fears of Europe' (Voltaire). However, 'the check to Colbert's policy, noticeable even in his lifetime, becomes conspicuously so after his death' (Hazard). The real nature of his achievement is still controversial.

Louis XIV gave war 'a higher priority than the fiscal stability and prosperity of his kingdom' (Ranum). The prospective gains from military glory were believed to be much greater. Under the influence of François-Michel Le Tellier, the Marquis de Louvois, a 'new militarism' was gradually seen to emerge. Not unexpectedly, war became one 'huge nationalised industry' (Pennington), and the army – its standing instrument – was ruthlessly and most efficiently reorganised. New concepts of fortification and new defence strategies were adopted under the direction of Sébastien Vauban, the French genius in military engineering. The king's glory and reputation in this field were equally enhanced by the professional art of diplomatic finesse in which his court is known to have excelled.

Louis XIV's foreign policy was characterised by four grandiose designs: the supremacy of the Bourbon House, the territorial aggrandisement and consolidation of his kingdom, political predominance in Europe and a universal recognition of pre-eminence for his defence of Christendom. The first war – the War of Devolution – has been compared to a 'triumphal procession', the French armies having met with hardly any effectual resistance. The Habsburgs were humiliated and France gained substantial territories in the east and north-east. It also created the first triple alliance which curbed Louis' rising ambition by forcing him to restore a part of his spoils. Or should one, perhaps, believe Louis XIV's later claim that he had preferred to be 'cautious and moderate' in May 1668 at Aix-la-Chapelle? Four years later France went to a prolonged war with the United Provinces, which ended with the incomparably prestigious statesmanship of Louis XIV at Nijmegen. But were not the peace treaties of 1678–9 also a triumph for his prime enemies, the Dutch, against whom he had declared the war six years earlier 'to destroy' them?

At this stage, observes Stoye, 'the achievement, and the prestige of the achievement, were such that they tended to make the monarchy impervious to its own defects, and they confirmed the primacy of foreign wars and foreign policy over domestic problems in the outlook of French statesmen.' *La raison du plus fort est toujours la meilleure*: this, backed by pseudo-legal claims, led Louis ostensibly on to proceed to 'a novel kind of conquest', the daring policy of 'peaceful' annexations, known as the *réunions*. Towns and territories, some of which were of significant strategic value, would be 'reunited' to the new France. These had hitherto been wrongly 'assumed to belong to Spain or to one or other of the states of the Empire' (Pennington). Louvois had purposely kept his armies after Nijmegen on a sound war footing. On the eastern frontiers of the Empire the militant Turks were laying siege to Vienna.

In 1685 Louis the Great revoked the Edict of Nantes. With one stroke of his pen, at Fontainebleau, the *religion prétendue réformée* ceased to exist in France, which soon became 'the scene of a persecution unparalleled since medieval times . . . [bringing] disorder, rebellion and an undeclared civil war' (Erlanger). Whether to appease Innocent XI over the *régale* dispute, or to realise his long-cherished dream of imposing a universal orthodoxy within his realm, this step was 'a colossal blunder' for which Louis had to pay dearly at home and abroad.

Foreign opposition grew steadily stronger. After the French atrocities in the Palatinate, it found formal expression in the powerful League of Augsburg. 'That such a coalition, on the scale of the Grand Alliance of The Hague (1674), could be formed in peace-time was a significant indication that Louis' disregard for European opinion had been carried too far, and that the initiative in Europe was slowly passing to his enemies' (Maland). A general European war broke out and after nine long years ended in Louis XIV's 'first great humiliation' at Ryswick. In the absence of the mighty Louvois, who died in 1691, Louis' military splendour had begun to dim. Soon his military glory and prestige, so aggressively and so provocatively won, would be diminished by defeats in the War of the Spanish Succession. His design for political preponderance in Europe had fallen apart. He died on 1 September 1715 and was 'conveyed to the basilica of Saint-Denis amid the abuse of a brawling, drunken populace, howling with barbaric joy' (Erlanger).

The long, costly span of incessant warfare, which marked the later reign, had impoverished France. It created problems and situations far too complex, too serious and too desperate for Colbert's inferior successors to solve. The king, absorbed in splendid isolation at Versailles, allowed the ties between his elaborate courtly world within the classical precincts of the new city and the provincial world beyond to be relaxed, almost to the point of complete severance. Away from the huge palace and its landscape gardening, millions of people lived the horrors of taxation, widespread economic depression, unjust privilege, religious intolerance and the notorious *dragonnades*. Here, men, women and children suffered, rioted, groaned and starved or froze to death. Louis had become a stranger to his people.

Yet, despite its many wars, despite its constraints and increasing discontent, the reign of Louis XIV had its 'credit side' too, which was 'just as extensive'. The intellectual and artistic flowering of France is what made the age of Louis XIV *le grand siècle*, and the Sun King's greatest legacy to posterity. 'Europe, or at least its élite,' claims Erlanger, 'became French by speaking the language, drawing inspiration from the creations and copying the customs of the land where the Great King reigned. Even among his bitterest enemies, there was not one prince whose descendants were not obsessed by his example. Because he succeeded in becoming both the sovereign and the patron of the great men of his age, Louis XIV left an indelible imprint on civilization.' He had almost destroyed France to have greatness thrust upon her.

'All I have by way of sources,' wrote Voltaire on his *Siècle de Louis XIV*, 'is some two hundred volumes of printed memoirs that everybody knows.' For the student of Louis XIV and France there is an embarrassing wealth of published source material, very often available in translation. This wide range of historical evidence includes collections of letters and diaries of a personal nature, originally meant to remain private; other diaries and memoirs which were intended from the start for publication; official government papers, correspondence and memoranda; ambassadors' and other eye-witnesses' reports; travel accounts and contemporary narratives of events. In approaching these and similar documents, the student should bear one important thing in mind. His analyses, comments and conclusions will inevitably reflect his preparation and further reading. '[T]he more knowledge a historian brings to the documents, the more knowledge they will impart to him. The historical process is thus one of asking questions as well as of recognition based on factual details' (Ranum).

I Every Inch A King

Introduction

The anarchy created by the Frondeurs demanded an unusually strong government to redress the balance. 'Authority must be established at any price and placed higher than before,' wrote Cardinal Mazarin in the *Carnets*, his secret diaries, in August 1648, 'or it will perish and be ridiculed and despised.' In 1661, at the age of twenty-two, Louis XIV, who ten years earlier had appeared to John Evelyn, the diarist, as the 'young Apollo . . . a Prince of a grave, yet sweete Countenance', assumed full, absolute authority over his kingdom. He had all the qualities of greatness and an implacable will to restore order and the dignity of the crown. 'I will die happy,' the Cardinal had once told him, 'when I see you prepared to govern by yourself, using your ministers only to present you with advice.' By 1661 the young monarch was well versed in 'the manners of royalty' and confident in 'the skills and deceits of statecraft'. Louis XIV was determined to be 'a true king, the opposite of a *roi fainéant*'. His long, direct personal rule was to be the realisation *par excellence* of Mazarin's desire. 'The proudest nobles put off their independence,' observes H. A. L. Fisher, 'lost contact with local affairs, and sank to the courtiers' level of intrigue, pettiness and servility.'

Though perhaps Louis XIV never uttered by word of mouth 'L'état, c'est moi', the way he spoke and the manner he acted left no doubt as to the priority the State held in his thought and deeds. Surrounded as much by 'servile flatterers singing endless eulogies' as by highly talented, disinterested and efficient public servants, he knew the amount of work and dedication the *métier du roi* necessarily entailed if taken seriously, how 'hard and vexatious' the tasks of royalty were. To Louis XIV kingship was an art, at once 'great, noble, and delightful', which he approached professionally, and from which he hardly ever relaxed.

Throughout France, royal authority radiated, like the sun, from Versailles, the hunting-lodge assiduously transformed into the splendid residence for the most fearful king in Europe, where glory and magnificence, splendour and spectacle were on permanent display. Divinely ordained, Louis 'claimed dominion over the property and persons of all his subjects', and considered himself omniscient and above the law. Freed of all traditional restraints, he enjoyed the liberty 'to tax at will' and, on more than one occasion, violated the fundamental laws of the kingdom. His brand of absolutism was defined by Cardinal de Retz as 'the most scandalous and dangerous tyranny'; his unorthodox style and methods of government elicited from Louis de Rouvroy, the enraged Duc de Saint-Simon, some of the most bitter criticism of the reign.

As the monarchy gradually tended to become more and more remote from the Parisians and the provincials, through 'psychological and institutional barriers', its *gloire* and the *bienfait* of the kingdom would eventually be seen to lose their one-time great and noble magic.

1 Authority must be established . . . higher than before

(a) *The king's journey from Paris*

You already know from the letters of Monsieur de Brienne, that the Queen has been compelled to leave Paris, and to secure the person of the King against certain sowers of dissension in the parliament. They purposed . . . to make themselves masters of his person, by
5   intelligences which they maintain with the enemies of the state, and at the same time by secret dealings with the people, all which has been further confirmed by subsequent events. In order then to cut off all means of injury from these raisers of disturbance, the King removed the parliament, but the younger advocates have hurried on
10   the older against their will to disobedience, and to so open rebellion, that they levy forces, excite the people to revolt, and place the King under the disagreeable necessity of inducing the inhabitants of Paris to obedience by force.

There is not a good Frenchman whose heart does not bleed for so
15   gross an attack upon the royal power, and that three or four seditious men should for their own advantage, bring the state from its high prosperity, to the verge of a precipice, unless God, who has hitherto protected the innocent King, should take him now under protection and avert so great a calamity. Yet this we may hope for from his
20   goodness, from the military power at our disposal, as also from the union of the royal family; although some princes and other great personages have embraced, on grounds of personal discontent, the party of the rebels. . . .

What wounds the hearts of their Majesties is that they must turn
25   their weapons against Frenchmen, and that the enemy gains by our disorders, nay, may, perhaps, obtain all the advantages of a long and glorious campaign. Then would the effusion of so much French blood and the expenditure of so much treasure be entirely useless, and we should be unable to conclude any peace with Spain which

30 should ensure the integrity of our provinces and the old boundary of
    the Rhine.

> Mazarin to Grignon, French ambassador in London, 23
> January 1649. Frederick von Raumer, *History of the Sixteenth
> and Seventeenth Centuries illustrated by Original Documents*,
> vol I (London, John Murray, 1835), pp 474–7

(b) The political state of France, 1655

At present no change is to be expected within the realm. The people,
so oppressed by misery, by the taille and by all sort of impositions,
would rather endure [these ills] than suffer war.

35 The nobility has been impoverished to such an extent that they
cannot attend any function on horseback, an appearance in some of
which would please them more than any betterment of condition.

The *Parlements* are totally subservient and those who compose
them do not dare to say anything against the present government.

40 The great cities do nothing but respire the peace and detest those
who were the authors of the latest troubles.

The ecclesiastical order is totally dependent on the court and on
the favoured ones from whom they have received their benefices.

All the *gouverneurs des places* are just as dependent on the court and
45 the Cardinal.

All the *grands seigneurs* do nothing but complain and I was not
acquainted with a single one of them who was capable of anything.

As for Paris the population detests the present government and yet
has subjected itself to it voluntarily. . . . One clearly sees that in
50 Paris the people desire calm and do not wish to listen to any more
bickering; this is certain.

As to the courtiers, they are constantly discontented but, in spite
of all this, the receipt of some sort of bounty appeases them, and
none of them is capable of doing anything.

55 [Even] the Maréchal de Turenne, who is the only one endowed
with sense, courage and experience, depends on favour, since after
his marriage he has fostered a great fear of losing his family fortune
and has become the valet of the Cardinal's valets. The other courtiers
are meaner than valets because they are slaves.

> Extract from an anonymous contemporary account. Public
> Record Office (London), State Papers Foreign, France
> (SP 78), vol 113, folios 48–9

Questions

a   Explain briefly the circumstances which 'compelled' the queen
    'to leave Paris'.

b   Explain and comment on the historical significance of Mazarin's
    reference to (i) 'certain sowers of dissension in the parliament'

(line 3) and 'these raisers of disturbance' (line 8); (ii) the 'peace with Spain' (line 29).

*   c   'They purposed . . . to make themselves masters of his person' (lines 3–4). How did 'subsequent events' (line 7) confirm Mazarin's claim?

  d   Whom, do you think, did Mazarin have in mind when he referred to 'some princes and other great personages' in lines 21–22?

  e   Explain the words in italics in extract b.

  f   From your knowledge of the period, do you find these two documents a fair comment on the state of France before 1661?

*   g   'Despite their discontents, the different classes of society were exhausted by the Fronde, and preferred their present state of subservience to a repetition of the futilities of the civil war' (Lough). In the light of this quotation, and with close reference to the second extract, discuss how the prevailing conditions in France in the 1650s helped to make possible the collapse of the Fronde and the final establishment of absolutism.

2   Royal Absolutism

(a)   The king's first act, 10 March 1661

Monsieur [Chancellor], I have called you, together with my secretaries and ministers of state, to tell you that up to this moment I have been pleased to entrust the government of my affairs to the late Cardinal. It is now time that I govern them myself. You will assist
5   me with your counsels, when I ask for them. Outside of the regular business of justice, which I do not intend to change, Monsieur the Chancellor, I request and order you to seal no orders except by my command, or after having discussed them with me, or at least not unless a secretary brings them to you on my part. And you,
10   Messieurs, my secretaries of state, I order you not to sign anything, not even a passport . . . without my command; to render account to me personally each day and to favour no one. . . . And you, Monsieur the Superintendent [of finances] I have explained to you my wishes; I request you to use M. Colbert whom the late Cardinal
15   has recommended to me. As for Lionne, he is assured of my affection. I am satisfied with his services.

  Quoted in J. B. Wolf, *Louis XIV* (Gollancz, 1968), p 133

(b)   Divine Right

[R]oyal authority is sacred . . . paternal . . . absolute . . . subject to reason. . . . God establishes kings as His ministers and reigns over people through them. . . . Therefore princes act as ministers of God
20   and as His lieutenants on earth. It is through them that He exercises

~1663

His empire. . . . The person of the king is sacred. . . . God has had
them anointed by His prophets with a sacred ointment, as He has had
His pontiffs and His altars anointed. But even before being in fact
anointed, they are sacred by virtue of their task, as representatives of
25 His divine majesty, delegated by His providence to execute His
design. . . .

Religion and conscience demand that we obey the prince. . . .
Even if kings fail in [their] duty, their charge and their ministry must
be respected. For Scriptures tell us: 'Obey your masters, not only
30 those who are mild and good, but also those who are peevish and
unjust.' Thus there is something religious in the respect which one
renders the prince. Service to God and respect for kings are one
thing. . . .

The prince need render account to no one for what he orders. . . .
35 When the prince has judged there is no other judgement.

> J. B. Bossuet, *Politique tirée des propres paroles de l'écriture
> sainte*, in *Oeuvres complètes de Bossuet*, ed. F. Lachat (Louis
> Vives, Paris, 1864–8), vol xxiii. This extract was written in
> about 1670 and first published in 1709

Questions

a   What important aspect of Louis XIV's character does the first
    extract reveal? In what ways was his 'first act' indicative of his
    new style of government? How revolutionary do you consider it
    to have been?
b   How does the second extract support the king's 'first act'?
★ c   How far, do you think, was Louis' success or failure dependent
    on his first batch of able ministers?
★ d   Who was Bossuet? How reliable and important are his writings
    as a primary source?
★ e   Was a defence of strong government really necessary in 1670?
★ f   Suggest possible reasons why Bossuet chooses to base his
    defence of absolutism on the Holy Scriptures rather than on
    'Roman Law or classical precedent'.
★ g   What dangers did the Theory of Divine Right Monarchy have in
    practice? When and in what ways were such dangers realised
    during Louis XIV's reign?

3 Nicolas Fouquet

(a) Louis XIV writes to his mother on the arrest. Nantes, 15 September 1661

Madame, my Mother, I wrote to you this morning of the execution
of my order for the arrest of the Superintendent [of Finances, Nicolas
Fouquet]; but I am now pleased to send you the details. You know

that for some time I have had it in my heart, but it was impossible to
5   do it earlier because I wanted him to pay the 30,000 *écus* for the navy,
and moreover it was necessary to adjust several other things that
could not be done in a day. You should have seen the difficulties I had
in speaking to d'Artagnan, for I was burdened with a crowd of
people, all of them alert, and they would have guessed my intention
10 at the slightest inclination. . . . Nonetheless, two days ago I ordered
him to be ready. . . . Finally this morning the Superintendent came
to work with me as usual; I received him in one way or another,
pretending to look for papers until I saw d'Artagnan through the
window in the court . . . [D'Artagnan] caught up with him in the
15 square before the church and arrested him on my order at about
noon. He demanded the papers that he carried, in which I am told
that I will find the true state of Belle-Isle . . . I have talked about the
incident with the gentlemen around me. . . . I told them frankly
that I had formed the project four months ago. . . . I told them that I
20 would not have another superintendent . . . that I would work on
the finances myself with the aid of faithful people who would act
under my direction, that this was the only true method of creating
[prosperity] and comfort for my people. You will have no trouble
believing that these people are sheepish, but I am satisfied that they
25 see that I am not so much of a dupe as they thought, and that it would
be wise to attach themselves to me.

*Lettre du roi Louis XIV écrit à la reine mère relative à l'arrestation
du Surintendant Fouquet.* Quoted in Wolf, op cit, p 141

(b) Madame de Sévigné to M. de Pomponne, 4 December 1664

At length the examinations are over. M. Fouquet entered the
Chamber this morning. The Chancellor ordered his *accusation* to be
read throughout. M. Fouquet spoke first upon the subject. 'I believe,
30 Sir,' said he, 'you can derive nothing from this document, but the
effect it has just produced, of overwhelming me with confusion.'
The Chancellor replied, 'You have yourself heard and seen by it, that
your regard for the State, which you have so much insisted upon in
Court, was not so considerable, but that you would have embroiled
35 it, from one end to the other.' 'Sir,' replied M. Fouquet, 'this idea
occurred to me only in the depth of the despair in which the Cardinal
often placed me; especially when, after contributing more than any
man in the world to his return to France, I found myself repaid by the
basest ingratitude. I had a letter from himself, and one from the
40 Queen–Mother, in proof of what I say; but they have been taken
away with my papers, as have several other letters. It is to be
lamented, that I did not burn this unfortunate paper, which had so
completely escaped my mind and my memory, that I have been
nearly two years without thinking of it, or knowing even that it

45   existed. However this affair may terminate, I disown it with my
     whole heart, and I entreat you, Sir, to believe, that my regard for the
     person and service of the King, has never been in the slightest degree
     diminished.' 'It is very difficult to believe this,' said the Chancellor,
     'when we see such contrary sentiments expressed at a different
50   period.' M. Fouquet replied, 'At no period, Sir, even though at the
     hazard of my life, have I ever abandoned the King's person; and, at
     the time in question, you, Sir, were at the head of the Council of his
     enemies, and your relations gave free passage to the army against
     him.'
55   The Chancellor felt this stroke; but our poor friend was irritated,
     and therefore not quite master of himself. The subject of his expenses
     was afterwards introduced. 'I undertake,' said he, 'to prove, that I
     have not incurred a single expense, which, either by means of my
     private income, with which the Cardinal was well acquainted, or my
60   appointments, or my wife's fortune, I was not able to afford; and if I
     do not prove this satisfactorily, I consent to be treated with the
     utmost ignominy.' In short, this interrogation lasted two hours; M.
     Fouquet defended himself ably, but with a degree of warmth and
     petulance; the reading of the *accusation* having ruffled him
65   exceedingly.

The Letters of Madame de Sévigné with an Introduction by
A. Edward Newton (London, W. T. Morrell, 1928), vol i,
pp 34–5

Questions

a   Identify (i) d'Artagnan (line 8) and (ii) Belle-Isle (line 17).
b   Why should the king have found it difficult to speak to
    d'Artagnan? Why was Fouquet dismissed and arrested? Suggest
    why the king had to wait for 'four months' (line 19) to execute
    such a 'project'.
c   Louis' letter to his mother has been described as 'a most
    interesting and revealing document' written 'from the King's
    own hand' (Wolf). What makes it 'most interesting' and what,
    do you think, does it reveal?
d   'Fouquet defended himself with courage' (Treasure). To what
    extent and in what ways does extract b convey this impression?
e   Fouquet's faults were the king's own. Is this a fair comment on
    Louis XIV?
f   Louis XIV's treatment of the Fouquet affair reveals in him a sign
    of weakness rather than strength. What arguments would you
    produce to confirm *or* refute this judgement?
g   'The plan of ruining him was laid with such odious art, and the
    conduct of his enemies, many of whom were his judges, was so
    inveterate, that it would have been impossible not to have been
    interested for him' (Newton). How far does the tone of Madame
    de Sévigné's letter support this view?

4 Métier du Roi

Kings are often compelled to act contrary to their natural inclination in a way that offends their own natural sense of right. They ought to give pleasure, and they often have to chastise and condemn people to whom they are naturally well disposed. The interests of the State
5 must come first. One has to overcome one's own inclinations, and not place oneself in the position of having to reproach oneself in important matters which might have been done better had not certain personal interests prevented it and turned aside the regard one ought to have had in the interests of the grandeur, the welfare, and
10 the power of the State.

There are often occasions which cause pain; some are delicate and difficult to unravel; one's ideas are sometimes confused. So long as that is the case, one can remain without coming to a decision; but the moment one has settled one's mind upon anything and thinks that
15 one has seen the best course, one must take it. That is what has often made me succeed in what I have done. The mistakes I have committed and which have caused me infinite pain, have been caused by obligingness and by letting myself surrender too heedlessly to the advice of others.

20 Nothing is so dangerous as weakness, of whatever kind it may be. To command others, one must rise above them; and after having heard all sides, one must decide on what must be done with an open mind, always keeping in view to order or execute nothing unworthy of oneself, of the character one bears, or of the grandeur of the
25 State. . . .

It is necessary to guard against oneself, against one's inclinations, and to be ever on guard against one's natural self. The role of King is great, noble and extremely pleasant, when one feels oneself worthy of acquitting oneself well in all things one sets out to do; but it is not
30 exempt from pain, exertion, and anxieties. Uncertainty sometimes makes one lose heart, and when one has spent a reasonable amount of time in examining a matter, one must come to a decision, and take the course believed to be best.

When one has the State in view, one is working for oneself. The
35 welfare of the one enhances the glory of the other. When the State is prosperous, eminent, and powerful, he who is the cause thereof is rendered glorious by it, and consequently must savour in a greater degree than his subjects of all that is most agreeable in life.

When one has erred one must mend one's fault as soon as possible,
40 and no consideration, not even kindness, must be allowed to prevent it.

Réflexions sur le métier du Roi, 1679. Bibliothèque Nationale (Paris), MS.Fr. 10331, folio 125 et seq.

Questions

a   From a close reading of this passage, arrive at your own definition of *métier du roi*.

★   b   'The mistakes I have committed' (lines 16–17). Suggest what Louis XIV had in mind when he made this 'confession'.

★   c   'Nothing is so dangerous as weakness' (line 20). How far, do you think, is it correct to say that behind Louis XIV's 'great deeds' lay an obsessive fear of failure?

d   'Indeed one does not expect a King to say notable things, but to do them' (Voltaire). In the light of this quotation, how far, do you think, is this extract reliable in order to assess Louis XIV's *real* performance?

★   e   In what ways do these 'reflections' show Louis 'firmly attached to the traditional principles of French absolutism'?

5   The State before affection

(a) The king to Colbert, 23 April 1671

I was master enough of myself the day before yesterday to conceal from you the sorrow I felt at hearing a man whom I have overwhelmed with benefits, as I have you, talk to me in the manner that you did.

5   I have been very friendly toward you; [and this] has appeared in what I have done. I still have such a feeling now, and I believe I am giving you real proof of it by telling you that for a single moment I restrained myself for your sake. I did not wish to say to you myself what I am writing you, not to give you a further opportunity to
10   displease me.

It is the memory of the services that you have rendered me, and my friendship, which made me act as I did. Profit thereby and do not risk vexing me again, because after I have heard your arguments and those of your colleagues, and have given my opinion on all your
15   claims, I do not wish to hear further talk about it, ever.

Now, if the Navy does not suit you, if it is not to your taste and you would prefer something else, speak freely; but after a decision that I give you, I wish no word of reply.

I am telling you my thoughts so that you may work on an assured
20   basis and take no false steps.

> Quoted in C. W. Cole, *Colbert and a Century of French Mercantilism* (Columbia 1939), vol i, pp 289–90

(b) The king on Louis François de Tellier, 29 October 1695

That the life your nephew has been following while at Fontainebleau is not suitable [to a secretary of state]; that the public is scandalised by it;

That his secretaries relax their efforts, following his example;

25 That officers of state cannot find him in office when they wish to speak to him; . . .

That he is given to deceptions; that he is always flirting; that he prowls everywhere, never staying at home; that everyone thinks he does not know how to apply himself to his work, seeing him forever

30 away from his office; . . .

That he arises late, spending the night dining out, often with princes; . . .

That if he does not have a complete change of heart, it will be impossible for me to retain him as secretary of state; . . .

35 That I would be sorry indeed to be forced to make changes but that I cannot avoid it;

That it is impossible that his duties can go well with so little application; . . .

That it is impossible that I could be deceived about so many

40 wrongdoings, especially about his lack of application to his duties; that his carelessness has cost me much;

That, finally, one simply cannot have conducted oneself in a more intolerable manner than he has;

That some say that I am to blame for his actions, especially at a

45 time like this, when the greatest and most important affairs are in his hands;

That I could not excuse myself if I did not interfere in these matters for the good of the state; indeed it is the good of the state that exonerates me;

50 That I am warning him, perhaps too late, but so that he may behave in a manner proper to his family's position; . . .

That [you] must make every effort to show [your] nephew the depths to which he has slipped and that he must agree to reform; that I do not want to lose the services of [your] nephew; that I have

55 affection for him; but that for me, the welfare of the state comes before everything else.

Letter by Louis XIV to the Archbishop of Rheims, uncle of Louis François de Tellier, Secretary of State for War. *Lettres de Louis XIV*, ed. Pierre Gaxotte (Paris, Jules Tallandier, 1930), p 98. Trans. by J. C. Rule

Questions

★ a Identify what you consider to have been the most important 'benefits' (line 3) with which Louis XIV had 'overwhelmed' Colbert.

★ b What 'services' (line 11) had Colbert 'rendered' Louis XIV by 1671?

c At times Colbert found it difficult to win 'the King's approval for his policies' (Lough). In the light of this statement, what aspects of Colbert's personality emerge from extract *a*?

d '[E]specially at a time like this' (lines 44–5). What does Louis mean?

e Suggest plausible reasons why Louis XIV did not dismiss Colbert and de Tellier for their 'misconduct' as he had done Fouquet.

f What do these two extracts suggest about Louis XIV's relations with his ministers?

6 The Qualities of Louis XIV

[A]lthough he is not brilliant, or very penetrating in his judgement, or very insightful, he has however enough good qualities to fulfil the duties of a great king. He is in good health; he has taste, discrimination, and sufficient shrewdness not to let himself be taken

5 by surprise; and he rewards merit when he finds it. Moreover, he is neither naturally sullen, nor quick-tempered, nor a scoffer, nor does he enjoy raillery at the expense of another person. This latter is a rare quality in a court and nation filled with men of this type. For one not learned or ever having devoted himself to study, or ever having been

10 attracted by it, he writes well and correctly. He loves the fine arts and promotes them; he is particularly knowledgeable about music, painting and building construction. He judges people and things sanely and fairly, in so far as he has some knowledge of them. He is master . . . of his *secret* . . .; he happily employs his *secret* as one of the

15 principal instruments to insure the success of his undertakings. . . .

His inclinations are naturally directed to uprightness, justice and equity, when they are diverted . . . by bad advice or by motives of interest, *gloire*, or, in a word, by the desire for the grandeur of his reign. He enjoys doing good by choice or impulse. . . . In addition,

20 the disorder in which he found the finances at the time of Cardinal Mazarin's death instilled in him a strong inclination for saving money and not for being extravagant, except for expenditures in such things as buildings. . . . Since he likes order, . . . and moderation, and since he is faithful to the duties of his religion and

25 practises them very regularly, he has, as a result, a well-regulated court and submissive courtiers. . . .

[However, t]he idea of his grandeur . . . preoccupies him, and he reflects more on the past successes of his reign than on the pretexts and means used to achieve them or indeed on the fortunate

30 circumstances which played an important part in shaping them. . . . Jealous in every way of his authority, sensitive otherwise to all that concerns it, or could endanger it, he is easily swayed to endorse the advice given to him and the measures proposed to sustain it. . . . This is the fatal source of the calamities and wars which surprised and

35 afflicted Europe several times and which ravage it today. Moreover, as he is more inclined to have his subjects regard him as a master than as a father, his reward is their submission and dependence rather than

their affection. He is not motivated by a real desire to relieve them
their miseries. . . . One needs only reflect, on the one hand, upon
40 the twenty-four millions that the chateau, the gardens, and the
fountains of Versailles cost, or on the work begun on Madame de
Maintenon's aqueduct, where more than thirty thousand men
worked for three years to direct, for a distance of sixteen leagues, the
water of a river into the reservoirs of Versailles. On the other hand,
45 one need only reflect on the misery of the common people and the
peasants, exhausted by the *tailles*, by having to lodge soldiers, by the
gabelles, and, finally, on the little care the king has taken to treat his
friends and allies kindly and to fulfil the obligations he should
undertake on their behalf.

> *Relation de France en 1690* by Ezcchiel Spanheim, the Elector
> of Brandenburg's envoy to the court of Louis XIV, ed.
> Charles Schefer (Paris, Renouard, 1883), pp 4–9. Trans. by
> J. C. Rule

Questions

a Louis had 'enough good qualities to fulfil the duties of a great
king' (lines 2–3). Which, according to Spanheim, were Louis
XIV's 'good qualities' and how far, do you think, were they
responsible for his 'greatness'?

b 'Fortunate circumstances' (lines 29–30). Identify these
circumstances carefully and explain their importance in 'shaping'
Louis XIV's 'successes' before 1690.

c Discuss the validity of what the author considers to have been
'the fatal source of the calamities and wars' (line 34) that 'afflicted
Europe' (line 35) during Louis' reign.

★ d What other sources would you use to confirm *or* refute the
evidence which Spanheim produces to support his claim that
Louis XIV was 'not motivated by a real desire to relieve [his
subjects] their miseries' (lines 38–9)?

7 Two Aspects of the King's Character

(a) Paris, Tuesday, 5 January 1672. Yesterday the King gave
audience to the Ambassador from Holland [Pierre Grotius]. . . .
The Ambassador presented his letter to the King, which was not
read, though the Ambassador proposed it; as the King said he
5 already knew the contents, having a copy of it in his pocket. The
Ambassador expatiated largely on the justifications mentioned in the
letter and on the strict manner in which the States had examined their
conduct to find out in what they could possibly have given offence to
His Majesty; that they were not conscious of ever having been
10 wanting in the respect that was due to him; and yet, to their great
surprise, they had heard that the extensive preparations His Majesty

was making were destined against them; that they were ready to satisfy His Majesty in everything he should be pleased to require from them, and humbly implored him to remember the good-will
15 his royal predecessors had ever shown them, to whom they owed their present flourishing condition. The King, with inimitable grace and dignity, replied, that he was not now to learn the endeavours that had been used to stir up his enemies against him; that he thought it but prudent to prevent a surprise, and that he found it necessary for
20 his own defence to make himself thus prepared and powerful by sea and land; that after giving a few more necessary orders, he should, in the beginning of spring, take such steps as he might judge most advantageous for his own glory, and the good of his kingdom; and then gave the Ambassador to understand, by a motion of his head,
25 that he would permit no reply.

(b) Paris, Wednesday, 13 January 1672. [L]et me give you an instance of the King's goodness and generosity, to show you what a pleasure it is to serve so amiable a master. He sent for Maréchal de Bellefonds, into his private room the other day, and thus accosted
30 him: 'Monsieur le Maréchal, I insist upon knowing your reasons for quitting my service. Is it through a principle of devotion? Is it from a inclination to retire? Or is it on account of your debts? If it be the latter, I myself will take charge of them, and inform myself of the state of your affairs.' The Maréchal was sensibly affected with this
35 goodness: 'Sire,' said he, 'it is my debts; I am overwhelmed with them, and cannot bear to see some of my friends, who assisted me with their fortunes, likely to suffer on my account, without having it in my power to satisfy them.' 'Well then,' said the King, 'they shall have security for what is owing to them: I now give you a hundred
40 thousand francs on your house at Versailles, and a grant of four hundred thousand more, as a security in case of your death. The hundred thousand francs will enable you to pay off the arrears, and so now you remain in my service.' That heart must be insensible indeed, that could refuse the most implicit obedience to such a
45 master, who enters with so much goodness and condescension into the interests of his servants. Accordingly the Maréchal made no further resistance: he is now reinstated in his place, and loaded with favours. This is all strictly true.

> Extracts from two of Madame de Sévigné's letters to her daughter Madame de Grignan. *Letters*, op cit, vol i, pp 30–1, 336

Questions

a Comment briefly on the circumstances which led to Pierre Grotius' audience with Louis XIV in January 1672.

★ b 'The good-will his royal predecessors had ever shown them, to whom they owed their present flourishing condition' (lines

14–16). Explain the historical significance of this observation and briefly discuss its validity.

c   Were the reasons given by the king for his 'extensive preparations' in the first extract justified?

d   What aspect of the king's character emerges from *each* of these two extracts?

★ e   'The fear of offending those in power, coupled with close police surveillance, should make us wary of placing too much trust in contemporary correspondence, including that of Mme de Sévigné' (François Dumont). In the light of this quotation, what reservations should a historian make in using accounts such as Madame de Sévigné's? What other sources would you consult to check the more important details in both extracts?

8   'Would I be King?'

(a) The king's day

As soon as he wakes, he recites the office of the Holy Spirit and his rosary; that being done, his preceptor enters for a study period . . . reading from Holy Scripture or the history of France. After that he gets out of bed and we [four members of the household] enter . . . he
5   then sits on the 'cut-out chair' in the alcove of the chamber . . . he then enters the grand chamber where usually there are princes and great lords who attend his *lever*. He is clothed in a dressing gown and goes before them speaking familiarly first to one then to another . . . which enchants them. After he has eaten his first breakfast, he
10   washes his hands, mouth, and face . . . takes off the cap that had been tied about his head because of his hair . . . he then prays to God in the passageway behind his bed, accompanied by his chaplains while everyone is on their knees, and if anyone dares to talk or make any noise a *huissier* removes him. The prayer of the King finished . . . he
15   does his exercises: he jumps to and fro with remarkable agility; then he rides his horse at full caper . . . and drills with the pike. After this he returns to the chamber where he dances. . . . He next goes back to his grand chamber where he changes clothes . . . then [he] goes up to the Cardinal's room . . . where a secretary of state makes his
20   reports on the most secret affairs of the King. . . . After that the King goes to greet the Queen . . . and then goes to hear mass. After mass he returns to his rooms, changes clothes, either to go on a hunt or to remain in the palace. If it is to be a hunt, he wears an ordinary hunting costume; if he stays, it is a modest one. . . . After dressing
25   he goes to dine, often with the Queen; sometimes after dinner there is an audience with ambassadors to whom he listens attentively.

'Fragments des Mémoires inédites de DuBois, Gentilhomme Servant du Roi' in *Bibliothèque d'école de Chartres*, vol ii, 4th series. Quoted in Wolf, op cit, p 90

(b) 'Too great a responsibility'

If it is an onerous task to find oneself responsible for a single family, and if it is bothersome to be answerable for oneself alone, how much more irksome is it to be responsible for a whole kingdom. Are the
30 prostrations of the courtiers in themselves an adequate remuneration for the tribulations of absolute power from which the sovereign is said to derive pleasure? I call to mind the devious and perilous ways which a sovereign is sometimes obliged to follow to maintain the public peace; I overlook the extreme but necessary means which he
35 frequently has to use for a good end: I know that he shall have to answer to God Himself as to the happiness of his subjects, that he is the dispenser of good and evil and that no amount of ignorance could constitute an excuse for him; so I ask myself: would I wish to be a king? Would a happy man, enjoying a private station in life,
40 renounce it for a crown? Is it not enough for the one who finds himself king by hereditary right to bear having been born royal?

La Bruyère, 'Du Souverain ou de la République', *Les Caractères* (Paris, L. de Bure, 1824), vol ii, pp 102–3

Questions

a How did the king divide his day? What other memoirists would you consult to confirm DuBois' picture?
b 'Contemporary opinion had it that Louis XIV was not very well educated' (Mousnier). What light does the extract shed on the nature of the king's education?
c Louis XIV 'seems . . . not to have taken his ideas from books but rather from observing his entourage and circumstances' (Mousnier). To what extent, and in what ways, does the first extract bear out this judgement?
d Who was La Bruyère and how reliable, do you think, are his writings as a source for a study of France under Louis XIV?
e On what evidence might a contemporary in 1688 (when *Les Caractères* was first published) have agreed with the subtle opinions expressed by La Bruyere in extract *b*?

9 Louis XIV's Courtiers

(a) At the royal chapel

The great persons of the nation assemble every day, at a certain hour, in a temple which they call a church. At the far end of this temple stands an altar consecrated to their god, where a priest celebrates the mysteries which they call holy, sacred and redoubtable. The great
5 ones form an enormous circle at the foot of this altar, and, standing erect, they turn their backs directly to the priest and the holy mysteries and lift their faces towards their king, who is seen kneeling

in a gallery, and upon whom they appear to be focusing their whole
heart and spirit. One cannot avoid seeing in this custom a kind of
10   subordination; for the people appear to be worshipping their prince,
while the prince [in turn] worships God.

> La Bruyère, 'De la Cour', *Les Caractères*, op cit, vol ii,
> pp 36–7

(b) A foreign nation?

The people of the court are like a foreign nation within the state,
made up of men drawn from many different places. They are not all
men of intelligence, but they are all possessed of an admirable
15   politeness which serves them in its stead. They are not all worthy
men, but they have the air and manner that make one think them
such. Their obliging and accommodating spirits can adopt any kind
of behaviour so that it is impossible to discover their true feelings.
Their contempt for anything that is not of the court is unimaginable
20   and goes to the point of extravagance. There is nothing well said or
well done, except what is said and done among them. Everything
that comes from outside is ignorant or boorish. It is however true
that, with the best taste in the world, they are for the most part
without any kind of learning, and they only make themselves out to
25   be knowledgeable in all manner of subjects by reason of a few
well-turned phrases and because of the respect they induce which
causes everyone else to fall silent in their presence.

> From *The Courtier's Mind*, written by the Abbé de Saint-Réal
> sometime towards the end of Louis XIV's reign. Quoted in
> J. Levron, 'Louis XIV's Courtiers', in *Louis XIV and
> Absolutism*, ed. Ragnhild Hatton (London, Macmillan, 1976),
> p 134

Questions

a   Compare the two extracts and explain what they reveal about the
courtiers' life under Louis XIV.
b   'The domestication of the nobles': how accurate is this
observation on La Bruyère's passage?
c   'The court became formal and depressing' (Levron): is this a valid
verdict to be drawn from Saint-Réal's picture?
d   Discuss briefly the tone of both extracts.
e   How far can a historian be sure that accounts such as extracts *a*
and *b* were truthful?

10   The 'Revolution' of 1661: a historian's view

The formula according to which 'the king governs through the
Grand Conseil' persisted under Louis XIV. But it had become a

myth, a fiction. Increasingly, it served as a mask to cover the reality, which was that decisions were being taken by one man – the king, the *contrôleur général*, one *commis* or another – or were the result of the deliberations of informal committees, where the decisive role was often played by the *rapporteur*. The councils became a magnificent façade. Officially, the government remained judicial in form. But the functions of government were now only partly carried out in the courts, less and less so as time went by. Quick and efficient, the executive form of government was well suited to the needs of warfare and so won out over the judicial. Executive government curtailed legal guarantees, however, and opened the way to arbitrariness and despotism, which, in the guise of parliamentarism, were to become the primary characteristics of French governments in the nineteenth and twentieth centuries.

This was a political revolution. It was also the beginning of a social revolution. The monarchy, and especially Louis XIV, eliminated some high crown officers, reduced the status of others, excluded from the councils all who were entitled to seats by virtue of their birth or position, diminished the role of the councils, and entrusted power to recently ennobled men rather than to the great families and their suites of vassals; they thereby broke the ties between the monarchy and the customary structure of French society. By changing, in fact, the political structure of the state, the traditional constitution of the kingdom, the monarchy also altered the distribution of power and, consequently, of influence and wealth within the social hierarchy, modifying the social hierarchy itself in the process. By giving precedence to fiscal concerns and to the fiscal spirit rather than to the ideas of dignity, honour (transmitted by birth more than acquired), and justice, the king undermined the society of orders. He thereby began the transition from a society of orders to a society of classes and from the absolute monarchy to the centralised bureaucratic state.

Roland E. Mousnier, *The Institutions of France under the Absolute Monarchy 1598–1789*, vol ii, *The Organs of State and Society*, trans. by Arthur Goldhammer (Chicago–London, 1984), p 159

Questions

a   Distinguish clearly between 'a society of orders' and 'a society of classes' (lines 32–3).

b   From your knowledge of the period, how accurate, do you think, is Mousnier's claim that 1661 marked a decisive turning point in the political history of France?

c   'It was also the beginning of a social revolution' (lines 17–18). What evidence does Mousnier produce to support his claim? What criticism can you make of this view?

II Power, Prosperity . . .

Introduction

'Il n'est force ni richesse,' writes Jean Bodin, 'que d'hommes.' In mercantilist thought man was the State's greatest reservoir of strength, power and wealth. With a stable demographic level of 18–20 million and covering (by 1700) some two hundred thousand square miles of land, France of the *grand siècle* was one of the most densely populated countries in Europe. It was also the most prosperous. Relatively rich in natural resources and with four-fifths of its inhabitants being peasants – 'productive' and 'taxable' – it enjoyed a material and military potential that was second to none and the envy of all.

During the first twenty years or so of Louis XIV's personal rule, French power and prosperity depended as much on the success and efficiency of his diplomatic machinery as on domestic peace and security. Louis' diplomatic service is said to have been the 'most dexterous in the world'. In diplomacy, as in any other branch of the art of kingship, Louis laid down, and very often followed, his own precept. 'Many monarchs,' we read in his *Mémoires*, 'would be capable of conducting themselves prudently in matters over which they had time to take counsel, who would not be equal to upholding their affairs by themselves in the face of accomplished and experienced ambassadors, who never come to them unprepared, and who always seek to take advantage of their masters.' As Ezechiel Spanheim and other foreign observers remark, during public and private audiences Louis XIV was, more often than not, discreet, firm and composed. However much Louis excelled at negotiations, it was perhaps to Hugues de Lionne's 'unrivalled knowledge of European politics' that France was deeply indebted for most of its monarch's triumphs 'in the early years of his reign' (Maland). What was the ultimate goal of Louis XIV's diplomatic machinery? Within the 'grand design' of Louis' foreign policy – 'the complete submission of Europe' to the *diktat* of Versailles – one wonders whether it was the task of his ambassadors to make peace and maintain a balance of power or to make enemies and create new antagonisms. Lavisse, in his *Histoire de France*, condemns Louis for breaking 'nearly every promise that he made'.

The army was indisputably of vital moment to the grandeur of

France. It was therefore necessary that military administration be drastically reformed on orderly lines. From 'a medley of armed levies', Michel Le Tellier and his son, the Marquis de Louvois, succeeded in remodelling the French army into a disciplined, efficiently organised and professional body. Colleges of military engineers were set up, siege-tactics improved, new weapons introduced and new methods of raising adequately and regularly paid armies were adopted. A prodigious amount of new defensive works began gradually to line the frontiers of France. Throughout his reign Louis XIV, 'a soldier-king to the end', remained excessively confident in his armies.

The economic prosperity of France of the *grand siècle* is generally attributed to the indefatigable work of Jean-Baptiste Colbert. 'Everything connected with finance,' writes Mousnier, was Colbert's 'province – that is, virtually the entire government'. He drastically reduced expenditure, controlled taxation not to exceed 100 million *livres* and did his utmost to make the entire fiscal system work uniformly. During his long administration, overseas trade flourished, colonisation received 'the full backing of the State', industrial development was revitalised and a system of patronage and pensions was introduced. From the 'few rotten hulks' of Mazarin's days, Colbert, to whom 'naval strength and economic prosperity were synonymous', created 'a powerful and well-trained navy' (De Wismes).

After more than three hundred years Colbert still remains a subject of controversy. T. K. Rabb calls him a 'great minister' and an 'innovative bureaucrat'. To what extent and in what ways, however, were his great reforms and innovations radical and structural? On the other hand, how fair is it to define his achievement as one 'limited to making the existing system function more efficiently' (Briggs)? There is at least one credit which may not perhaps be denied Colbert: he had 'diagnosed the sickness which threatened to destroy French greatness: that of idleness' (F. Deyon).

Under the monarchy of Louis XIV two worlds coexisted – Versailles and France. They were two distinct realities. The world of the Sun King, of Lionne, Le Tellier, Louvois, Colbert and 'that narrow circle of rich idlers' was the world of the court at Versailles. But 'France,' says Ashley, 'was not the Court':

> The true France was represented by the soldiers who manned the entrenchments at Malplaquet, the sailors who punished the Mediterranean pirates and conquered the great de Ruyter, the savants who sailed to Siam happily discussing philosophy, the prosperous bourgeoisie depicted by Molière, the hard-working administrators and diplomatists, the peasants and craftsmen who made French decorative arts and food and wine famous throughout the civilised world. The greatness of France lay in men and things like these, and the Court of Versailles was merely the passing symbol of their glory.

1 France's demographic level

Généralité	Population
Town of Paris, 1694	720 000
Généralité of Paris, 1700	856 938
Généralité of Orleans, 1699	607 165
5 Généralité of Tours, 1698	1 069 616
Brittany, 1698	1 655 000
3 généralités of Normandy, 1698	1 540 000
Picardy, 1698	519 500
Artois, 1698	214 869
10 Flemish Flanders	158 836
Walloon Flanders, 1698	337 956
Hainaut, 1698	85 449
Trois-Evêches	156 599
Champagne, 1698 (includes Sedan and	
15 part of Luxembourg)	693 244
Généralité of Soissons, 1698	611 004
Burgundy, 1700 (includes Bresse, Bugey	
and Gex)	1 266 359
Lyonnais	363 000
20 Alsace, 1697	245 000
Dauphiné, 1698	543 585
Provence, 1700	639 895
Languedoc, 1698	1 441 000
Roussillon	80 369
25 Auvergne, 1697	557 068
Généralité of Bordeaux, 1698 (includes	
Bigorre, Labour and Soule)	1 482 304
Béarn and Basse-Navarre, 1698	241 094
Généralité of Montauban, 1699	788 600
30 Généralité of Limoges, 1698	585 000
Généralité of La Rochelle, 1698	860 000
Généralité of Poitiers	612 621
Généralité of Moulins	324 332
Total according to Vauban	19 094 146

'Abstract of the Census of the People of the Realm', drawn up
by Sébastien Vauban in 1707. Quoted in Pierre Goubert, *The
Ancien Régime: French Society 1600–1750* (London,
Weidenfeld & Nicolson, 1973), p 45. Trans. Steve Cox

Questions

   a Explain '*Généralité*' and say which one has been inadvertently left out by Vauban. Why, do you think, is the 'total' given 'according to Vauban' (line 34)?

★ *b* Which geographical parts of France appear most densely populated from Vauban's data? How were these related to the country's pattern of economic development during Louis XIV's reign?

   c Vauban's collation of demographic data has been called 'speculative'. Suggest how these estimates could have been obtained.

   d About 80 per cent of France's population was rural 'both in its habitat and employment'. What implications does this observation have on interpreting Vauban's 'census'?

   e During Louis XIV's reign France's demographic level was 'two or three times' higher than 'any other state' in Europe. What material advantages did the French monarchy derive from such a situation?

★ *f* Statistics such as Vauban's should be treated with great caution. What major difficulties does a demographic historian have to face in the course of his research?

2 In search of markets overseas

Those who wish to go to Martinique, Guadeloupe and to the other islands of America either for settlement or for working at their trade will be transported and fed on the aforesaid ships according to the customary manner for the sum of fifty livres each, one half to be paid
5 immediately and the other six months after their arrival at the above mentioned islands.

    Those who wish to establish dwellings on the above mentioned islands will also be provided with as much land as they can cultivate and have cultivated. Moreover, these lands will be granted without
10 any payments and with exemptions from all obligations for three years. The Company will likewise furnish and advance wood, materials, negroes and beasts.

    For those who prefer to go to the aforementioned island of Cayenne than to Martinique, Guadeloupe, and the other islands and
15 will engage themselves in the service of the Company for three years, they will be transported and fed for the above length of time. They will have the customary wages, and if they desire to reside there at the end of the above three years, they will be given as much lands in ownership as they are able to cultivate.
20   The artisans and craftsmen who voyage to Cayenne or the other islands of America will be considered as masters in such towns of France where they wish to live after they have practised their arts and

crafts in America during the time set down by the grant and verified
by the Parlement. Tools will be supplied to those who do not have
25   them.

The inhabitants of the above mentioned islands and the mainland
of America for their advantage will be able to export to France all the
goods which they extract from the exploitation of their lands and to
import from France foodstuffs, goods and merchandise which they
30   need for the maintenance of their families and residences on the
vessels of the Company. To facilitate the sending and receiving of
such goods and merchandise the Company will acquit them of all
import and export tolls for the payment of a reasonable sum which
would cover both the freight of the merchandise and the demands of
35   the tolls.

All artisans, craftsmen, or manual labourers who wish to be
engaged in the service of the Company in the aforementioned lands
and those who wish to travel in the aforementioned ships to establish
residence there should present themselves in the office of the General
40   Directors situated in Paris or in the seaports to the directors and
commissioners for the Company, who have sufficient authority to
agree with applicants over the above conditions which will be
punctually executed.

Done at the office of the General Directors of the West India
45   Company in Paris, the eighth day of August 1664.

> Reproduced and translated in F. C. Lane, 'Colbert and the
> Commerce of Bordeaux', in *Venice and History: The Collected
> Papers of Frederic C. Lane* (Baltimore, Johns Hopkins, 1966),
> pp 319–20

Questions

a   Make a list of the main incentives aimed at encouraging the
     Bordelais to settle on 'the islands of America'. What, do you
     think, made such 'conditions' attractive to potential applicants in
     1664?

b   Discuss briefly the reasons for Colbert's apparent enthusiasm for
     extending trade and developing colonies.

c   What light does this document shed on Colbert's overall
     commercial policy?

3 Colbert's Ideal

(a) *Colbert's memorandum to Louis XIV, 1670*

[Your Majesty] has undertaken a war of money against all the states
of Europe. He has already conquered Spain, Italy, Germany,
England and some others, in which he has caused great misery and
want, and by despoiling them he has enriched himself. Only

Holland is left, and it fights with great reserves: its commerce with the North, which brings it so many advantages and such a great reputation for its sea forces and navigation; that of the East Indies, which bring it every year 12m in cash; its commerce with Cadiz and that with Guinea and an infinity of others in which its strength consists and resides. . . . This war, which consists only in wit and energy, and of which the spoil of the most powerful republic in Europe must be the prize of victory, cannot soon be finished. Or, to put it better, it should be one of the chief objects of the application of Your Majesty during his whole life.

> Document reproduced in Cole, op cit, vol i, (New York, p 343)

(b) A historian's view

Thus commerce – and here Colbert spoke his mind – was 'a war of money'.

He repeated this expression very often. This was his war, here he was Louvois. It was his wish that this should be the war preferred by the King. . . . The thought was an obsession. . . .

Colbert understood the great natural advantage France possessed 'in the position in which Providence had placed her'. If she made the effort, if 'to the natural strength of France, the King was able to join that which the art and the industry of commerce could produce, only the slightest reflection on the strength of cities and states who had only a fraction of that art and industry, would enable one to judge that the grandeur and power of the state would augment prodigiously. . . . The art and industry of commerce', that is to say the work of production and the work of marketing, were accordingly obligations of subjects to the State, in the nature of civil duties. In a well-ordered state there should be none but workers. . . .

'In so far as possible the different professions of your subjects ought to be restricted to those which can serve these great purposes. These are agriculture, trade, the army and the navy. . . . If Your Majesty could limit all of his people to these four kinds of pursuits, one could predict that he would be able to be master of the world.' . . .

[O]bstacles, very numerous and of all kinds, stood opposed to efficient labour: the lack of communications, internal tariffs, the diversity of customs of weights and measures; the poor rural economy, peasants who did not know 'what their soil was best suited for', and who, besides, were discouraged, ruined by taxes and by all sorts of vexations and injustices. Added to all this were the cities burdened by debt, without hope of solvency; municipalities in the hands of privileged classes who scorned manufacturing. Many trades were abandoned; products which France had exported in other days were at present purchased abroad. Almost nothing remained of our merchant marine or of our fighting fleet.

This picture of a great country in ruin was put before Louis XIV
50 by Colbert a hundred times. . . .

He dreamed of an entirely different France . . . a France which was self-sufficient, imposing its will on other nations, enriched by the influx of gold, and, victorious in the war of money, sustained against all other peoples, rising superbly amidst the ruin of others. . . .
55 Colbert offered his ideal to France, but feared its rejection.

Ernest Lavisse, *Histoire de France depuis les Origines jusqu'a la Révolution*, vol vii (Paris, Hachette, 1905); reproduced in translation in *Readings in European Civilization since 1500*, ed. Richard H. Powers (Boston, 1961), pp 134–6

Questions

a What do these extracts tell us about Colbert? To what extent do you find Colbert's argument for the extension of trade convincing?

b Suggest reasons why Colbert overdoes, perhaps deliberately, the military imagery in the first extract?

c Explain (i) 'a war of money' (lines 1 and 15–16); (ii) 'here he was Louvois' (lines 17–18); (iii) the advantage France possessed 'in the position in which Providence had placed her' (line 21).

★ d '[A] great country in ruin' (line 49): is this a fair description of France before the accession of Louis XIV?

★ e 'Colbert offered his ideal to France' (line 55): suggest reasons why he 'feared its rejection' (line 55). To what extent and in what ways was Colbert's 'dream' eventually realised?

4 The Provincial Intendants

(a) *Colbert to de Creil, Intendant for Rouen, 27 January 1673. De Creil had just 'become involved in a conflict with the Cour des Aides of Normandy' (Mousnier)*

His Majesty, as always unwilling to allow any impediment to his authority, a portion of which he has vested in you, has quashed the decree of the Cour des Aides and forbidden the court and the *avocat général* to promulgate its like in the future. However, His Majesty
5 has further ordered me to write you that, in the light of the explanations that you yourself have provided for each article, he deems you to have been wrong on nearly every count; he has determined that you had set up your own court before which *avocats* and *procureurs* appeared along with the parties and that either you
10 yourself or your subdelegates had assumed jurisdiction over cases normally lying within the jurisdiction of the *élus* and the Cour des

Aides. To which he has ordered me to add that, if you do not change your conduct in this regard and adopt a diametrically opposite course of action, he will be unable to retain you in your position.

(b) Colbert to de Sève, Intendant for Bordeaux, 18 May 1674

15 I cannot refrain from pointing out to you that what most pains the King in the conduct of the *commissaires* he has dispatched to the provinces is their establishment of large numbers of subdelegates in all the localities of their departments. They then attribute to these subdelegates, on their own authority, the authority to assume
20 jurisdiction over all sorts of affairs, quite often abusing their own authority in the process and extending their authority as their fantasies, passions, and interests may dictate.

On this point I must tell you that the subdelegates that you have introduced are a very great abuse, established by the *commissaires*
25 without reason, ground, or necessity. In all the provinces they are a universal source of complaint, complaint that frequently reaches the eyes and ears of His Majesty. It is true that your commission gives you the power to name subdelegates. But the king's intention and the primary use of this power were never for affairs of brief duration
30 to which you were unable to attend because a number of affairs claiming your attention happened to arise at the same time. I therefore think it my duty to advise you that nothing you could do would be more agreeable to His Majesty than to reduce the number of subdelegates and only to make use of them in the manner that I
35 have just explained.

Pierre Clément, *Lettres, instructions et mémoires de Colbert* (Imprimerie Impériale, Paris, 1861–82); extract *a* in vol ii, pt 1 no 232, p 266; extract *b* in vol iv, no 98, p 108. Both extracts reproduced in R. Mousnier, op cit, vol ii, pp 521, 523–4

(c) Colbert to Le Vayer, Intendant for Soissons, 22 November 1682. 'A declaration of 23 February 1677 had ordered that writs served on taxpayers by bailiffs, "sergents", and "archers" be sent for inspection within four days to the "bureaux des Finances" or "élections". In order to speed up the collection of tax revenues, Le Vayer invoked a council decree of 27 January 1670 as grounds for interfering in this inspection' (Mousnier)

The declaration of 1677 contains the express law established by the king in regard to the inspection of writs. It was sent to *parlement*, registered, and notified to all the courts, and there is therefore no question that it abrogates all previous laws on this subject.
40 Jurisdiction in the matter belongs to the regular judges, and you were not authorised and should not have interfered without express

authorisation issued subsequent to the date of this declaration. This is the invariable rule of the kingdom's universal justice, particularly as it applies at present in the area of finance, which is intended to
45   leave the regular judges jurisdiction over matters normally within their purview until such time as they may abuse their authority. The function of the intendants and *commissaires* in the provinces is only to see to it that the judges do their duty and execute the laws and ordinances established by the Prince, and if they should fail to do so,
50   to advise the Council of such failure. They are not to assume direct jurisdiction over any affairs other than those for which they have been granted specific power by the King.

Cited in R. Mousnier, op cit, vol ii, p 522

Questions

a   Why is Colbert reprimanding each of his three intendants? What, do you think, is his main objective in these letters?
b   How do these letters bear out the general attitude of Louis XIV's government to the provincial intendants?
c   'The king in no way wished to set up a nationwide network of subdelegates' (Mousnier). How would you use the source material in these letters to explain and support this claim?
★ d   '[A] portion of which he has vested in you' (line 2). What functions, other than those specified in Colbert's letters, were the provincial intendants expected to perform? How important were the intendants during and after Colbert's ministry? What light do they shed on Louis XIV's system of government?

5   The French Navy

[Louis XIV] was as assiduous in his efforts to secure the sovereignty of the seas as he had been to form numerous and well-trained armies upon land, even before war was declared. He began by repairing the few ships that Cardinal Mazarin had left to rot in the ports. Others
5   were bought from Holland and Sweden, and in the third year of his government he despatched his maritime forces in an attempt to take Jijeli on the coast of Africa. In 1665 the Duke of Beaufort began to clear the seas of pirates, and two years later France had sixty warships in her ports. This was only a beginning, but while in the midst of
10   making new regulations and fresh efforts, he was already conscious of his strength, and would not allow his ships to dip their flag to the English. It was in vain that King Charles II's council insisted on this right, which the English had acquired long since by reason of their power and labours. Louis XIV wrote to his ambassador, Count
15   d'Estrades, in these terms: 'The King of England and his chancellor may see what forces I possess, but they cannot see my heart. I care for nothing apart from my honour.' . . .

Meanwhile the work of establishing a navy capable of upholding such arrogant sentiments progressed everywhere. The town and
20 port of Rochefort were built at the mouth of the Charente. Seamen of all classes were enrolled, some of whom were placed on merchant vessels and others distributed among the royal fleets. In a short time sixty thousand were enrolled.

Building commissions were set up in the ports so that ships might
25 be constructed on the best possible lines. Five naval arsenals were built at Brest, Rochefort, Toulon, Dunkirk and Hâvre-de-Grâce. In 1672, there were 198 ships of the line and 40 frigates. In 1681, there were 198 ships of war, counting the auxiliaries and 30 galleys in the port of Toulon . . .; 11,000 of the regular troops served on the
30 ships, and 3,000 on the galleys. 166,000 men of all classes were enrolled for the various services of the navy. During the succeeding years there were a thousand noblemen or young gentlemen in this service, carrying out the duties of soldiers on board ship, and learning everything in harbour to do with the art of navigation and
35 tactics. . . . [These] have since proved themselves a school which has produced the finest ships' officers in the navy. . . .

The naval forces greatly assisted in protecting trade. The colonies of Martinique, San Domingo and Canada, hitherto languishing, now flourished, and with unhoped-of success; for from 1635 to 1665
40 these settlements had been a burden upon the nation.

In 1664, the king established a colony at Cayenne and soon afterwards another at Madagascar. He sought by every means to redress the folly and misfortunes which France had brought upon herself by ignoring the sea, while her neighbours were founding
45 empires at the ends of the world.

Voltaire, *The Age of Louis XIV*, trans. by Martyn P. Pollack (London, Dent, 1926), pp 331–3

Questions

★ *a* How justified are Voltaire's references (lines 3–4, 39–40, 43–5) to the state of the French navy before the accession of Louis XIV?

    b Explain the historical significance of Voltaire's reference to the English in lines 11–17.

    c What general impression of Colbert's naval reorganisation do you get from this extract? Is there any significant gap in Voltaire's account?

    d Discuss briefly, with close reference to the extract, the navy's contribution to the grandeur of France under Louis XIV.

★ *e* 'When it came to deciding upon priorities Louis XIV was to neglect the fleet for the army' (Treasure). In the light of Voltaire's account and from your knowledge of the period, to what extent and in what ways, do you think, is this judgement tenable?

6 The French Army: John Locke's Impression

Paris, 5 January 1679. This day was the review of the infantry of the Maison du Roy, for soe the horse & foot guards are called. There were 30 companys, if one may recon by their colours, of French & 10 of Swisse, all new habited, both officers & soldiers. The officers of
5 the French gold or for the most part silver imbroidery or lace in blew, & the Swisse officers all gold on red & much the richer.

The French common soldiers all in new clothes, the coats & breeches of cloth almost white, red vests laced with counter fait silver, lace under or at least as much of it as was seen before was red
10 cloth, though if one looked farther, one should have found it grafted to linin. Shoulder belt & bandeleirs of buffe leather laced as their vests, red stocking & new shoes. A new hat laced, adorned with a great white, woollen feather, though some were red. A new paire of white gloves with woollen fringe, & a new sword, copper gilt hilt.
15 All which, I'm told, with a coat to wear over it of a grey stuff, cost but 44 livres, which is bated out of their pay, out of which, all defalcations being made, there remains for their maintenance 5 s. per diem. The soldiers, as I over tooke them comeing home to Paris, had most of them oiled hat cases too, a part, I suppose, of their furniture,
20 & coorse, linin buskins after the fashion of the country to save their red stockings.

The Swisse soldiers were habited in red coats & blue britches cut after their fashion, with their points at the knees, & had noe feathers. The pike men of both had back & breast [plates], but the Swisse had
25 also head pieces which the French had not. For the Swisse the King pays each captain for him self & all the men in his company 18 livre per mensem, which is all their pay, but the captain's profit lies in this, that he agrees with his officers as he can per mensem & soe with the soldiers, who have some 9, some 14 £ per mensem & soe between as
30 they can agree.

The French colours were in a field azure sprinkled flowerdelys or a crosse argent charged at every end with a crown or. Thus they were all but one, which was azure 4 crowns or. The Swisse colours were a crosse argent, the 4 cantons, filld with stropes of yellow, azure &
35 red, wavy, all pointing to the center of the crosse.

As the King passed at the head of the line as they stood drawn up, the officers at the heads of their companys & regiments in armer with pikes in their hands saluted him with their pikes & then with their hats, & he very courteously put off his hat to them again, & soe he
40 did again when, he taking his stand, they marched all before him. He passed twise a long the whole front of them forwards & backwards, first by himself, the Dauphin etc., accompanying him, & then with the Queen, he rideing along by her coach side.

John Locke's travels in France 1675–1679, ed. J. Lough (Cambridge University Press, 1953), pp 254–5

   a Distinguish between the French and Swiss guards of the 'Maison du Roy'.

   b 'An extraordinarily imposing sight'. To what extent and in what ways does Locke's account convey this impression?

   c By the 1670s the French army no longer remained the 'irregular and shabby force' it had been before the accession of Louis XIV. What evidence can you adduce from this extract in support of this claim?

★   *d* 'These troops . . . were at once the terror and admiration of people to whom every kind of splendour was unknown' (Voltaire). Is this statement justified?

7 The Lyons Silk Industry

[T]o understand [fully] the rise of the Lyons silk industry it is not sufficient to study only its quantitative and technical aspects – one must also use that wider approach typical of the art historian to appreciate many aspects of the development of a French fabric

5   industry which was able to achieve a degree of independence, even though Italian influence continued to be felt. And in Lyons' bid for success, design proved the winning card. Although Avignon could boast good technical expertise and a large output of finished silks and fabrics, the creation of a group of designers whose task was to bridge

10   the gap between painting and weaving was entirely the work of Lyons. We do not know precisely when it was that a distinction began to be made between the weaver and the designer in preparing a new fabric, nor about how the division of labour was organised. The employment of professional designers was all the more necessary

15   since a whole range of artists, including some of the most famous of their time, took a direct interest in applied art. The influence of painting on textile design brought with it quite new styles which differed from the traditional Italian decorations. . . . The most important contribution of the Lyons industry lay in the introduction

20   of new motifs and new ways of representing nature. The passion for pomp and splendour flourished under the absolute monarchy, floral motifs were eagerly taken up, with branches and foliages that were larger than life. The naturalist craze was just beginning, and with it the predominance of French design in silk textiles. . . . The

25   designers also looked to the technical aspects of weaving, and if they did not all invent new technical methods of weaving . . . they had certainly many new suggestions and ideas to put forward. . . . Lyons, in fact, provided an excellent and rewarding meeting-place

30 for technical and economic development, on one hand, and artistic innovation on the other.

Salvatore Ciriacono, 'Silk Manufacturing in France and Italy in the XVIIth century: Two Models Compared', *Journal of European Economic History* (Banco di Roma), X, no 1 (Spring 1981), pp 184–5

Questions

a   Explain (i) 'quantitative and technical aspects' (line 2); (ii) 'a degree of independence' (line 5); (iii) 'division of labour' (line 13).
b   What 'wider approach' is suggested in line 3?
c   Distinguish between the 'weaver' and the 'designer' in the preparation of 'a new fabric' (lines 12–13).
d   Suggest how Louis XIV's absolute monarchy could have stimulated the silk industry at Lyons.
★ e   'The naturalist craze was just beginning' (line 23). Explain the historical significance of this observation.
★ f   In the light of the last sentence (lines 28–30), discuss briefly the importance of Lyons as a focal point of French commerce.

8   An Evening at Versailles

I was on Saturday at Versailles with the Villars. . . . [T]hat fine apartment of the King's . . . is furnished with the utmost magnificence; they know not there what it is to be incommoded with heat; and pass from one room to another without being
5   crowded. A game at *reversi* gives a form to the assembly, and fixes everything. The King and Madame de Montespan keep a bank together. Monsieur, the Queen, and Madame de Soubise, Dangeau, and Langlee, with their companies, are at different tables. The baize is covered with a thousand louis-d'ors; they use no other counters. I
10   saw Dangeau play, and could not help observing how awkward others appeared in comparison to him. . . . I bowed to the King in the way you taught me; and he returned my salutation, as if I had been young and handsome. The Queen talked to me of my illness, nor did she leave you unmentioned. The Duc paid me a thousand of
15   those unmeaning compliments, which he bestows so liberally. . . . You know what it is to receive a word from everyone who passes you. Madame de Montespan['s] . . . beauty and her shape are really surprising; she is much thinner than she was; and yet neither her eyes, her lips, nor her complexion, are injured. She was dressed in
20   French point; her hair in a thousand curls, and the two from her temples very low upon her cheeks; she wore on her head black ribbons, intermixed with the pearls, which once belonged to the Maréchale de l'Hôpital, diamond pendants of great value, and three or four bodkins. In a word, she appeared a triumphant beauty,

25   calculated to raise the admiration of all the foreign Ambassadors. She
has heard that complaints were made of her having prevented all
France from seeing the King; she has restored him, as you see, and
you cannot imagine the delight this has occasioned, nor the
splendour it has given to the Court. This agreeable confusion,
30   without confusion, of all the most select persons in the kingdom,
lasts from three o'clock till six. If any couriers arrive, the King retires
to read his letters, and returns to the assembly. There is always
music, to which he sometimes listens, and which has an admirable
effect: in the meantime, he chats with the ladies. . . .
35   At six they take the calèshes; the King and Madame de
Montespan, the Prince and Madame de Thianges, and Mademoiselle
d'Heudicourt, upon the little seat before, which seems to her a place
in Paradise. You know how these calèshes are made; they do not sit
face to face in them, but all look the same way. The Queen was in
40   another with the Princesses: the whole Court followed in different
equipages, according to their different fancies. They went
afterwards in gondolas upon the canal, where there was music: at ten
the comedy began, and at twelve they concluded the day with the
Spanish entertainment of *media noche*; thus we passed the Saturday.
      Madame de Sévigné to Madame de Grignan, Paris,
Wednesday, 29 July 1676. *Letters*, op cit, vol iii, pp 281–3

Questions

a   Identify (i) *each* person mentioned in lines 6–8, with the exception
of the king and the queen; (ii) the Maréchale de l'Hôpital (line 23);
(iii) 'the canal' (line 42).

b   Explain briefly the *reversi* game (line 5).

★ c   Suggest what Madame de Sévigné had in mind when she referred
to the 'complaints' made about Madame de Montespan's 'having
prevented all France from seeing the King' (lines 26–7). How
valid, do you think, were these 'complaints'?

d   What impression of (i) Madame de Sévigné, (ii) life at Versailles,
do you get from a close reading of this letter?

e   'Her portraiture may seem casual but it is very perceptive'
(Treasure). What qualities of Madame de Sévigné as a writer does
this letter reveal?

9   Life in the Provinces

(a) The Rocks [in Brittany], Wednesday, 5 August 1671. You shall
now have news about the [Provincial Estates], as reward for your
being a Breton. M. de Chaulnes [Governor of Brittany] made his
entry on Sunday evening, with all the noise that Vitré could afford;
5   the next morning he sent me a letter, which I answered by going to
dine with him. There were two tables in the same room, at one of

which M. de Chaulnes presided, and his lady at the other. There was a great deal of good cheer, whole dishes were carried away untouched, and the doors were obliged to be made higher, to admit the pyramids of fruit. Our ancestors had certainly no notion of these machines, since they simply imagined, that if a door was high enough for themselves to enter, it was sufficient. A pyramid was to make its entry; one of those, for instance, that oblige you to haloo from one end of the table to the other; but so far is this from being an inconvenience in this part of the world, that you are often very well pleased at not seeing what they conceal. This pyramid, with about twenty or thirty pieces of china on it, was so completely overturned at the door, that the noise it made silenced our violins, haut-boys, and trumpets. After dinner Messieurs de Lomaria and Coëtlogon danced some excellent jigs with two Breton ladies, and minuets in a style that far exceeded anything I have seen at Court; their Bohemian and Lower Breton steps were danced with a lightness and exactness that charmed me. . . . I am sure you would have been delighted with Lomaria's dancing; the music and *passe-pieds* at Court are really sickening in comparison.

(b) The Rocks, Wednesday, 19 August 1671. I left this good town [of Vitré] last Monday, after having made your compliments to Madame de Chaulnes, and Mademoiselle de Murinais. . . . All Brittany was drunk on that day. We dined apart. Forty gentlemen dined in a lower room, each of whom drank forty toasts: the King was the first, and then the glasses were broken. All this was done under pretence of extreme joy and gratitude for a hundred thousand crowns which His Majesty had remitted out of the free gift the Province [of Brittany] had made him, as a recompense for their having so cheerfully complied with his request. So now there is only two million two hundred thousand livres, instead of five hundred thousand.

Madame de Sévigné to Madame de Grignan, *Letters*, op cit, vol i, pp 236–7, 248–9

Questions

a Explain (i) 'Provincial Estates' (line 2); (ii) 'these machines' (lines 10–11).

b Explain, and comment briefly on, the historical significance of the occasion described in extract *b*.

c According to Madame de Sévigné, how different, do you think, was aristocratic life in the provinces from that at Versailles?

★ d 'She knew that her daughter showed her letters to friends' (Durant). With reference to these and other extracts in this book from Madame de Sévigné's letters, discuss briefly the value of her 'sprightly recounting of trifles' (Voltaire) to the historian.

★ e Madame de Sévigné's 'letters are a commentary upon Louis XIV's reign seen from the angle of a woman on the fringe of the court, sufficiently in touch to be accurately informed, but never so close to events as to become *blasé* or to lose her sense of fun' (Treasure). With close reference to these and other extracts from her letters quoted in this book, how far, do you think, is this an accurate observation?

10 Paris in 1698: an Englishman's view

I viewed the city [of Paris] in all its parts and . . . I must needs confess it to be one of the most beautiful and magnificent in Europe, and in which a traveller might find novelties enough for six months for daily entertainment. . . .

5   'Tis also most certain, that for the quantity of ground possessed by the common people, this city is much more populous than any part of London; . . . here the palaces and convents have eat up the peoples' dwellings, and crowded them excessively together, and possessed themselves of far the greatest part of the ground; whereas
10   in London . . . the people have destroyed the palaces, and placed themselves upon the foundations of them, and forced the nobility to live in squares or streets in a sort of community: but this they have done very honestly, having fairly purchased them. . . .

The houses everywhere are high and stately; the churches
15   numerous, but not very big; the towers and steeples are but few in proportion to the churches, yet that noble way of steeple, the domes or cupolas, have a marvellous effect in prospect. . . .

All the houses of persons of distinction are built with porte-cochères, that is, wide gates to drive in a coach, and consequently
20   have courts within; and mostly remises to set them up. . . .

As the houses are magnificent without, so the finishing within side and furniture answer in riches and neatness; as hangings of rich tapestry, raised with gold and silver threads, crimson damask and velvet beds, or of gold and silver tissue. Cabinets and bureau's, of
25   ivory inlaid with tortoishell, and gold and silver plates, in a hundred different manners; branches and candlesticks of crystal; but above all, most rare pictures. The gildings, carvings and paintings of the roofs are admirable.

These things are in this city, and the country about, to such a
30   variety and excess, that you can come into no private house of a man of substance, but you see something of them . . .

It may very well be, that Paris is in a manner a new city within this forty years. 'Tis certain since this king came to the crown, 'tis so much altered for the better, that 'tis quite another thing. . . .
35   The streets are lighted alike all the winter long, as well when the moon shines, as at other times of the month . . .

After all, it must be said that this magnificence, and the number of these palaces and gardens, are the best and most commendable effect of arbitrary government. If these expences were not in time of peace, what would be this king's riches, and the extream poverty of the people? For it is said that every three years . . . he has all the wealth of the nation in his coffers; so that there is a necessity he should have as extravagant and incredible ways of expending it, that it may have its due circulation amongst the people.

But when this vast wealth and power is turned to the disturbance and destruction of mankind, it is terrible; and yet it hath its use too: we and all Europe have been taught, by the industry of this great king, mighty improvements in war; so that Europe has been these twelve years an over-match for the Turk; and we for France by the continuation of the war.

> Dr Martin Lister, *A Journey to Paris in the Year 1698*, third edn (London, 1699), in *The Century of Louis XIV*, ed. Orest and Patricia Ranum (London, Macmillan, 1972), pp 215, 216, 220, 223, 235

Questions

  a How accurate is the distinction between Paris and London in the second paragraph?

★ b From your knowledge of the period how justified, do you think, is Dr Lister's claim that 'since this king came to the crown' (line 33) Paris was 'so much altered for the better' (lines 33–4)?

★ c Comment on the historical accuracy of the author's argument in lines 37–44.

★ d Suggest what the author meant by his reference to 'mighty improvements in war' in line 48.

★ e What evidence would you produce in support of the statements in lines 48–50, 'so that Europe . . . war'?

III . . . Poverty and Problems

Introduction

Louis XIV's thirst for glory, his incessant wars and the crippling amount of taxes which he extorted to be able to realise his 'grand design' reduced the peasants of France to abominable conditions. Jean de la Bruyère, an accurate contemporary observer of manners, writes:

> One meets with certain wild animals male and female scattered over the country, dark, livid and tanned by the sun, bound to the soil that they till with invincible obstinacy; they have something like an articulate voice and, when they rise to their feet, they reveal a human face. They are in fact men. At night they retire to their hovels where they live on black bread, water and roots.

His passion for grandeur and authority, observes Saint-Simon, had 'smothered all other considerations within him'. A recent historian remarks that Versailles

> was more than a folly, more than a preposterous and extravagant display of personal glory. It was consciously designed to dazzle Europe and to tame the French aristocracy. As such it succeeded, beyond all doubt. At the same time, it cut off the leaders of French society, including the king himself, from the people they ruled. The court . . . bore little relation to the world of ordinary men and women except in so far as they were taxed . . . to maintain it. All this glory was built on the backs of the peasants, and no account of Louis XIV's achievement would be complete that put in Versailles but left out this other France in which incessant toil, poverty and starvation were daily realities. (R. Lockyer)

Compared with the enormous social and economic changes that occurred during the Renaissance and the Reformation, it is debatable how rapid a development France had experienced under Louis XIV. 'Many of the new industries established by Colbert,' Lough argues, 'did not have a lasting success, as they were unable to survive the expulsion of the Huguenots and the crushing taxation of the second half of the reign.' Madame de Sévigné's letter of 31 May 1680 provides insight into the backward system of internal communications and the poor state of the roads. Transport remained 'primitive', while the *péages* and the *trailes* kept hampering domestic trade. The merchant class never carried with it any social esteem. Moreover, very 'little was done' for agriculture. It seems that Colbert had never realised that the French economy was predominantly agrarian, with the consequence that 'the peasant was left to fight his own struggle for existence unaided' (Maland). During Louis XIV's personal rule, 'much or all' of France experienced three major *crises de subsistence*: 1661–2, 1693–4, which was perhaps the 'heaviest' in 'mortality', and 1709–10.

Louis XIV was oblivious to the sufferings of the ordinary French man and woman; and this in spite of 'the greatest pains' he took 'to be informed of all that happened everywhere, in public places, in private houses, in social life, in the privacy of families and intimacies' (Saint-Simon). 'For most of his subjects,' says Briggs, 'the reign of the Sun King was an epoch of hardship, often of despair and untimely death.' The monarch had been unable, writes Ashley, 'to deal drastically with the pressing problems of the mass of his subjects'. Michelet describes France at the end of the *grand siècle* as financially and morally bankrupt. Louis XIV, claims Lavisse, had 'exhausted' France.

1   The problem of poverty

(a) Colbert, 1670

During the course of this year I find the abundance which was apparent everywhere has changed for two very compelling reasons. . . . The first is the increase in expenditures, which are climbing to 75 million, and which consequently exceed revenues by
5   5 million in peace time. The other is the general difficulty which the tax farmers and the *receveurs généraux* are having in getting money out of the provinces, the delays in their payments to the royal treasury, and their daily protestations with the enormous poverty which they find in the provinces makes them fear their financial ruin
10   and that they will not be able to keep up the payments of their tax farms and of the general taxes.

This situation can be accepted as all the more truthful since we know clearly through various accounts that poverty is indeed very great in the provinces, and although it may be attributed to the small
15   demand for wheat, it is clearly apparent that some other more powerful cause must have produced this poverty, even though the failure of wheat sales could indeed prevent farm workers from having enough money to pay their *tailles*; but whatever the case may be, when money is in the kingdom the universal desire to make
20   profit from it makes men set it in motion, and it is by this motion that the public treasury finds its share. And thus, there is necessarily some

other cause for this poverty than the failure of the wheat market. . . .

All that the people can save up is divided into three portions: the first, what they can set aside for their subsistence and for their small savings; the second for their masters, who are the owners of the land which they cultivate; and the third, for the King. This is the natural and legitimate order of this distribution. But when authority is at the point where Your Majesty has put it, it is certain that this order changes, and that the *peuple*, who fear and respect this authority, begin by paying their taxes, set aside little for their subsistence, and pay little or nothing to their masters. And since these people must have the wherewithal to pay before they think of meeting their tax obligations, and since their taxes must always be proportionate to the money that each individual may have, the general financial administration must always be watchful and exercise all the care and all Your Majesty's authority in order to attract money into the realm, to spread it throughout the provinces in order to make it easy for the *peuple* to live and pay their taxes.

> 'Mémoire au Roi sur les finances', in *Lettres, Instructions et Mémoires de Colbert*, ed. Pierre Clement (Paris, 1870), vol vii, reproduced in translation in Ranum (eds), op cit, pp 113, 114

(b) Boisguilbert, 1697

In effect, the arbitrary *taille* compels a merchant to hide his money, and a farmer to let his land lie fallow, for if one wishes to do business and the other to plough they would alike be crushed with the *taille* by powerful men, who themselves are in the position of paying little or nothing.

The *aides*, customs, and taxes on goods coming in and out of the kingdom (all of them four times as heavy as the goods can support) bring it about that a man sees his cellars full of wines rotting, whilst they are very dear in his neighbourhood, so that five hundred millions are lost to the revenue of the kingdom.

Must peace be awaited before it is possible to save the lives of at least two or three thousand creatures who perish every year from poverty, especially in childhood, half of them not being able to grow to the age when they could make their own living since their mothers lack milk through shortage of food and excess of work; while at a greater age, having only bread and water, without beds, clothes or any remedies for their illnesses, deprived of sufficient strength to work, which is their only source of income, they perish before completing half their life.

> Pierre Le Pesant, Sieur de Boisguilbert (*lieutenant général* for Rouen and surrounding district), *Détail de la France*, ed. E. Daire (Guillaumin, 1843), quoted in translation in H. G. Judge, *Louis XIV* (Problems and Perspectives in History) (London, Longmans, 1965), p 104

a Explain (i) *receveurs généraux* (line 6); (ii) 'the arbitrary *taille*' (line 40); (iii) *peuple* (lines 30, 39); (iv) *aides* (line 45).

b To what extent and in what ways was 'abundance . . . apparent everywhere' (lines 1–2) in France before 1670?

c In the light of the second extract, how valid, do you think, are Colbert's 'two very compelling reasons' (lines 2–3) why 'abundance . . . has changed'?

d 'But when authority is at the point where Your Majesty has put it . . .' (lines 28–9). How far was the superstructure of monarchical power the root of all the poverty in the provinces during the personal rule of Louis XIV?

e Compare and contrast the concept of poverty as entertained by Colbert in 1670 with that of Boisguilbert in 1697.

2 Against Mercantilism

(a) God by His Divine Providence, wanting not only to bestow everything which may serve to bring about the felicity of His creatures, but also desiring to create amity and a universal society . . . has diversified lands and climates so each country produces
5 something . . . not common elsewhere. And wishing to exchange surplus for [products] more rare, a country must have recourse to that universal correspondence and mutual exchange which we call commerce. It is simple to understand that by blocking entry [of goods] with impositions so excessive as to prohibit their sale, a
10 country prevents its subjects from easily enjoying that which is grown elsewhere and also stops them from exchanging or selling their own products, in this way compelling people to remain encumbered with things they have in overabundance while rendering them at the same time incapable of procuring that which
15 they need.

> 'Mémoire de M. de Groot, Ambassadeur d'Holland', reproduced in translation in Lionel Rothkrug, *Opposition to Louis XIV: The political and social origins of the French Enlightenment* (Princeton, N.J., Princeton University Press, 1965), pp 206–7

(b) Monsieur Colbert should beware that by wanting to put France in a position to dispense [with the trade] of all other peoples, that, on their side, they do not think of doing the same. It is certain they have taken another route and have gone elsewhere to obtain most of the
20 things with which they used to furnish themselves in our Provinces. One of the principal causes of the scarcity of money which we see in France in the midst of so great an abundance of grain and wine proceeds from [the fact] that the Dutch no longer come and

discharge [France of her surpluses] as they did previously, because
25 our conduct towards them in matters of commerce makes them see
clearly that we will take nothing from them in exchange. . . . We
propose to oblige them to pay us entirely in cash.

> Anon., *Mémoires pour servir à l'histoire D.M.R. avec quelques
> réflexions politiques sur les mémoires* (n.p., 1668), reproduced in
> translation in Rothkrug, op cit, pp 201–2

Questions

a 'Monsieur Colbert should beware' (line 16). What light do these
two documents shed on Colbert's ideal of 'a war of money' (cf.
Section II, No. 3)?
b 'One country could only expand its trade, and hence its general
prosperity, at the expense of others.' How would you refute this
mercantilist belief by using the source material in extracts *a* and *b*?
c Assess briefly the historical validity of the specific references in
extract *b* to conditions in France in 1668.

3 La Fontaine: 'La mort et le bûcheron'

A poor old Woodman with a leafy load,
Both with his faggots and his years bowed down,
Groaning, with heavy steps along the road
Laboured to reach his hovel smoked and brown.
5   At last, with toil and pain exhausted quite,
He dropt the boughs to muse upon his plight.
What pleasure had he known since he was born?
In th' whole round world was any more forlorn?
Often no bread, never an hour of rest:
10   His wife, his children, soldiers foraging,
Forced labour, debt, the taxes for the King –
The finished picture of a life unblest!
He called on Death, who instantly stood by,
And asked of him: 'What is 't you lack?'
15   'I wanted you,' was the reply,
'To help me load this wood upon my back.'

> *La Fontaine's Fables* (London, Dent, 1952), trans. Edward
> Marsh, p 17

Questions

a Discuss briefly La Fontaine's attitude towards his Woodman. In
what ways does this reflect the social status of the French peasant?
b La Fontaine's *La mort et le bûcheron* is 'a vivid picture of the
sufferings of the poorer type of peasant'. Comment briefly on the

historical significance of each of the burdens, listed in the fable, which the peasant had to bear in seventeenth-century France.

c   What effects did these burdens have on French agriculture in general?

* d   The study of history enhances one's appreciation of literature. In what ways can the study of seventeenth-century French literature help the historian to understand the *grand siècle* in all its vitality and diversity?

4 John Locke's conversation with a peasant woman

Talking in this country with a poor peasant's wife, she told us she had 3 children; that her husband got usually 7s. per diem, finding himself, which was to maintain their family, 5 in number. She indeed got 3 or 3½s. per diem when she could get work, which was
5   but seldom. Other times she span hemp, which was for their clothes and yielded no money. Out of this 7s. per diem they 5 were to be maintained, and house rent paid and their *taille*, and Sundays and holy days provided for.

For their house, which, God wot, was a poor one room and one
10   storey open to the tiles, without window, and a little vineyard which was as bad as nothing (for though they made out of it 4 or 5 tierce of wine – 3 tierce make 2 hogheads – yet the labour and cost about the vineyard, making the wine and cask to put it in, being cast up, the profit of it was very little) they paid 12 *ecus* per annum rent and for
15   *taille* 4 *livres* for which, not long since, the collector had taken their frying pan and dishes, money not being ready.

Their ordinary food rye bread and water. Flesh is a thing seldom seasons their pots, and, as she said, they make no distinction between flesh and fasting days; but when their money reaches to a more costly
20   meal, they buy the inwards of some beast in the market and then they feast themselves. And yet they say that in Saintonge and several other parts of France the peasants are much more miserable than these, for these they count the flourishing peasants which live in Graves.

Locke's 'peasant woman', according to John Lough, was 'the wife of an agricultural labourer of the wine producing region of Graves, near Bordeaux'. Lough, op cit, pp 236–7

Questions

a   What impression of the peasants of the Graves region do you get from this 'conversation'?

b   In 'Saintonge and several other parts of France the peasants are much more miserable' (lines 21–2). What light does this observation shed on the general plight of the French peasantry?

How reliable, do you think, are such observations, based on
what 'they say' (line 21)?

c   What conclusions would you draw from this impression on the
splendour and magnificence of the court of Louis XIV?

d   For the courtiers of Versailles the peasant was simply 'a beast of
burden'. To what extent is this a fair judgement on the peasant's
lot during the *grand siècle*?

5   Widespread vagrancy

On 22 December 1684 in a secluded village in the Cevennes, it is
freezing hard. Gabriel Georges, a vagrant, is breathing his last in the
poor-house. He dies, and his body is buried in a special cemetry for
poor outsiders. Where had he come from? By his own account, he
5   was forty-six years old, born in La Familiere, in Poitou. His fate was
typical: working through the death-registers and poor-house
records, one continually comes across these vagrants heading
southward towards the sun and the Mediterranean, their entire
baggage consisting of a small pot for boiling soup and collecting
10 coins. . . . Tramps turned rag-pickers, they collect old clothes and
germ-laden rags, vectors of all kinds of diseases, and send them to
paper mills. . . . With the onset of winter they go to earth in barns
and *métairies*, to be turfed out by the farmhands in the early morning,
stiff with cold, sometimes frozen to death. Others are locked up in
15 the poor-houses and are racked with hunger when fed upon a kind of
greyish unleavened bread, as in Montpellier. . . . But until about
1700 their way of life was characterised much more by tramping
than confinement: the watch, gate-keepers, *chasse-coquins* and
magistrates . . . try in vain to put them behind bars. All those who
20 share the old persuasion, and still believe, as in medieval times, that
beggars are a chosen race – small fry, lackeys, the livery, children,
nuns, inn-keepers or prostitutes – protect them, rescue them from
the clutches of the *chasse-gueux*, harbour them and set them free
again: thus in Montpellier in 1685, a woman named Gasconne, a man
25 named Barbe and a nun named Carabosse are fined for harbouring
beggars. . . . A parish of any importance will see scores or hundreds
of vagrants passing through every year; the Montpellier poor-house
alone handed out over forty thousand '*passades*' in sixty-five years.
They haunt the churches in jostling throngs but people claim that
30 they will not pray; they offend the faithful with their stink and
noise. . . . They take up residence on threshing-floors and
farmyards, in barns and tileworks, woods and huts. They walk into
people's houses . . . murder and steal; call themselves soldiers but
produce no discharge; feign mutilation; form begging bands of four
35 or more . . . carry muskets, pistols, bayonets and iron-shod staves;
dog the path of great worthies, the king and the Estates, so that they

leave a long malodorous wake of squalid poverty and beggary. . . .
It does no good to alternate kicks with ha'pence, shave and flog them
in tandem, sometimes shoot them down . . . burn their flea-ridden
40   bedrolls or drive them twenty miles away on carts or mule-back
'amid popular acclamation'. Nor to send them on their way in more
humane fashion with a bowlful of soup or a spoonful of beans and a
piece of black bread, shared with a few lepers. They always return.
        Emmanuel Le Roy-Ladurie, *Les Paysans de Languedoc*
        (S.E.V.P.E.N., 1966), quoted in Pierre Goubert, *The Ancien
        Régime: French Society 1600–1750* (London, Weidenfeld &
        Nicolson, 1973), trans. Steve Cox, pp 115–16

Questions

a   Explain (i) the words in italics; (ii) 'their way of life was
    characterised much more by tramping than confinement' (lines
    17–18).
b   From information provided, or implied, in this passage, discuss
    briefly the social composition of the vagrant 'class'.
c   What are 'the death-registers' (line 6) and the 'poor-house
    records' (lines 6–7)? For what reasons are such sources useful to
    the historian? What other sources would you consult for reliable
    information about vagrants?
d   What conditions, do you think, encouraged vagrancy in Louis
    XIV's France?
e   The 'Church, the State, town councils and provinces had been
    campaigning since the mid-seventeenth century for the "great
    confinement" (le *grand renfermement*)' of vagrants (Goubert). To
    what extent, do you think, was this 'an indication of social fear
    rather than organisation'?

6   The famine of 1693 in the village of Rumegies

[T]he final misfortune was the utter failure of the ensuing harvest,
which caused grain to reach a tremendous price. And since the poor
people were exhausted in like measure by the frequent demands of
His Majesty and by these exorbitant taxes, they fell into such
5   poverty as might just as well be called famine. Happy the man who
could lay hands on a measure of rye to mix with oats, peas and beans
and make bread to half fill his belly. I speak of two thirds of this
village, if not more . . .
        Throughout this time, the talk was all of thieves, murders and
10   people dying of starvation. I do not know if it is to the credit of the
curé of Rumegies to refer here to a death which occurred in his parish
during that time: a man named Pierre du Gauquier, who lived by the
statue of the Virgin, towards la Howardries. This poor fellow was a

widower; people thought that he was not as poor as he was; he was
15 burdened with three children. He fell ill, or rather he grew worn-out
and feeble, but nobody informed the *curé*, until one Sunday, upon
the final bell for mass, one of his sisters came and told the *curé* that her
brother was dying of starvation, and that was all she said. The pastor
gave her some bread to take to him forthwith, but perhaps the sister
20 had need of it for herself, as seems likely to be the case. She did not
take it to him, and at the second bell for vespers the poor man died of
starvation. He was [not] the only one to drop dead for want of bread,
but several others died of that cause a little at a time, both here and in
other villages, for that year saw a great mortality. In our parish
25 alone, more people died than in several ordinary years. . . . Men of
goodwill had their hearts wrung at the sight of the poor people's
sufferings, poor people, without money while a measure of corn
cost nine to ten *livres* at the end of the year, with peas and beans
corresponding. . . .
30 The ordinance made by His Majesty (on 20 October 1693) for the
relief of his poor people cannot be forgotten here. . . . Every
community *had to* feed its poor. The pastors, mayors and men of law
taxed the wealthiest and the middling, each according to his
capability, in order to succour the poor, whom it was also their duty
35 to seek out. . . . In this village, where there is no court and
everybody is his own master, the *curé* read out and reread that
ordinance to no avail. The *mayeurs* and men of law, who were the
richest and would therefore have to be taxed most, fought it with all
their might. With much hardship, August was finally reached. A
40 fortnight beforehand, people were harvesting the rye when it was
still green, and putting it in ovens to dry it, and because this grain
was unripe and unhealthy it caused several serious illnesses. May the
Lord in his fatherly Providence vouchsafe us to be preserved
henceforward from a like dearth.

> *Journal d'un curé de campagne au XVIIe siècle*, ed. Henri Platelle
> (éditions du Cerf, 1965), reproduced in Goubert, op cit,
> pp 47–8

Questions

a   What does the author mean by 'the frequent demands of His
Majesty' in lines 3–4?

b   'In this village . . . everybody is his own master' (lines 35–6).
What light does this remark shed on the absolute government of
Louis XIV?

c   'Mortality' seems very often to have been more the result of
exorbitant prices than of scarcity of food. In the light of this
observation, what conclusions would you draw on (i) the general
economic mechanisms in France (ii) the socio-economic
conditions of the majority of Frenchmen?

d Why should 'a tremendous price' of grain give rise to widespread 'starvation'? What impression of the general diet of the French population do you get from this phenomenon?

7 Vauban's 'Dîme royal', 1698

(a) The Maréchal de France's inquiry into the conditions of the people

I say it with all imaginable sincerity, that it is not out of any fondness of my own abilities, nor any inclination to arrogate to my self any thing above my merit, or to attract any additional esteem, that I have set about this work. I am neither a scholar, nor one concerned with
5   the revenues; and should I attempt to acquire honour or profit by things that do not belong to my profession, I should do it with a very ill grace. I am a *French* man, well affected to my country, and very sensible of the distinguishing marks of favour the King has been pleased for a long time to heap upon me. . . .
10   The wandering life I have led for above forty years has given me opportunities of seeing and observing, often and in different manners, the most part of the provinces of this kingdom. . . . The state and condition of the people, whose poverty having often moved my compassion, has put me upon an enquiry into the causes
15   of it. . . .
During the several years that I have made it my business to enquire into that matter, by all I can observe and find, in these late times, near a tenth part of the people are actually reduced to beggary; but of the other nine parts, not five of them are in a condition to give alms to
20   that tenth, by reason of the miserable condition they are reduced to, and the small pittance that is left them. That of the four other parts of the people, three are in hard circumstances, by reason of their great debts, and the inextricable law-suits they are intangled in; and that of the other tenth part, in which I comprehend the gentlemen of the
25   sword (as they are called), those of the robe, both clergy and laity, the nobility of all sorts, all those who bear civil or military offices, the rich merchants and burghers that have estates, and others who are pretty well to pass; I say, of all those there cannot be reckoned above a hundred thousand families. And I should not be much out of
30   the way if I averred, that, great and small together, there are not ten thousand of them whose circumstances are easy; and if you will abstract from those the farmers of the revenues, under-farmers, collectors, etc., and all their associates and adherents, open and secret, and those the King maintains by his favour, some few
35   merchants, etc., I am very sure the remainder would be small.
Though the causes of the misery of the people of this kingdom be well known . . . it would be a thing of great use and importance to

find out some substantial remedy for this evil, now while we enjoy a
peace, which promises us a long continuance. . . .
40   In effect, the establishment of a Royal Tithe, laid upon all the fruits
of the earth, on one hand, and on all that produces yearly incomes on
the other, seems to me to be the most equal and proportional of all
other; because the one goes always with the land, which yields
increase according to its fertility; and the other goes according to the
45   evident and unquestionable incomes. This scheme is of all other the
least liable to corruption, because it is subject only to its own
regulations, and does in no way depend on the will and pleasure of
any man.
        S. Vauban, *A Project for a Royal Tithe, or General Tax*
        (London, 1708), extracts from the Preface, pp i–viii

(b) Saint-Simon on Vauban's book

It was full of information and figures, all arranged with the utmost
50   clearness, simplicity and exactitude. But it had a grand fault. It
described a course which, if followed, would have ruined an army of
financiers, of clerks, of functionaries of all kinds: it would have
forced them to live at their own expense, instead of at the expense of
the people, and it would have sapped the foundation of those
55   immense fortunes that are seen to grow up in such short time. This
was enough to cause its failure. All the people interested in opposing
the work set up a cry. . . . What wonder, then, that the King, who
was surrounded by these people, listened to their reasons, and
received with very ill grace Maréchal Vauban when he presented his
60   book to him.
        *Memoirs of the Duc de Saint-Simon on the Times of Louis XIV and
        the Regency* (Washington, 1901), vol i, p 372

Questions

a   Explain the historical context of, and comment on, the
     following: (i) 'the distinguishing marks of favour . . . upon me'
     (lines 8–9); (ii) 'The wandering life I have led for above forty
     years' (line 10); (iii) 'now while we enjoy a peace' (lines 38–9).
b   What was the overall purpose of Vauban's 'enquiry'?
c   Comment briefly on the historical significance of 'This scheme
     . . . any man' in lines 45–8.
d   From your knowledge of the period, show how truthful or
     otherwise are Vauban's 'findings' in the third paragraph of
     extract *a*. What other sources would you consult to check their
     validity?
e   Why, according to Saint-Simon, did Vauban fail 'to convert the
     authorities' to his views? How does the tone of Saint-Simon's
     argument reflect his 'genuine sympathies' for 'the people'?

f How does the source material in both extracts reflect upon the grandeur of Louis XIV's monarchy?

8 The economic crisis: a historian's view

The whole period 1660–1730 is characterised by a general fall in prices and incomes. This fall, sometimes gradual, sometimes abrupt, with occasional brief moments of stabilisation, is the symptom of a prolonged economic depression. It is certain that the
5 production and prices of textiles in Picardy and the Beauvaisis both fell disastrously at this time and there was a feverish search for new markets; such symptoms in industry are in no sense the mark of a period of prosperity. In terms of population, the losses incurred in 1647 to 1653, followed by another heavy drain in 1661 to 1662, were
10 to have serious consequences for a number of age-groups over the next twenty years or more. After the decade 1680–90, when normal fertility was about to lead to another upward movement, the heavy mortalities of 1691–4 and 1709–10 intervened; then the number of burials increased three- or four-fold above normal and the birth-rate
15 was gradually depressed, leading to a profound disturbance of the age-composition of the population for nearly fifty years to come. Except in the first years of Colbert's ministry the tax burden on the country side continually increased, particularly after 1690. During the same period the French coinage became progressively debased. It
20 is true that the peasantry, into whose economy money scarcely entered, suffered only indirectly from successive devaluations; but the drastic reorganisation of the *seigneuries* held by the bourgeoisie and clergy, accompanied by a general overhaul of the registers of landed property and more accurate land surveys, led, in practice, to
25 an increase in seigneurial dues, which fell mainly on the countryside. The condition of the peasantry under Louis XIV is, in fact, the product of an exceptional convergence of unfavourable factors. Those writers who were aware of economic developments and had a direct knowledge of the country as a whole – men like Hevin and
30 Boisguilbert, and reformers, Vauban above all – pointed to, and even exaggerated, the fall in agricultural incomes, the decline of ground-rents, the stagnation of industry, and the general impoverishment of the peasantry. By and large this was the picture presented by the Beauvaisis, which never quite recovered from the
35 long crisis of the mid-century. One is tempted to talk of an atrophy or general stagnation of the countryside. Suddenly, around 1694 and 1710, catastrophic increases in prices and poverty, which drove up still further the endemic burden of peasant debt, led to yet another transfer of thousands of acres of plough-land to the bourgeoisie,
40 who, at the same time, completed the ruin of the last remnants of the old nobility of the Beauvaisis. This time, too, the great abbeys took

part in the kill. It is true that the reign of Louis XIV ended, for the majority of the peasantry of the Beauvaisis, in the unhappy manner described in the orthodox textbooks. But in the midst of the general
45 distress, the powerful caste of the big *fermiers-receveurs* attained its highest point of wealth, social power and arrogance. More sharply than before, peasant society became split into distinctive groups with conflicting interests and outlooks. Though the general picture is one of decline, the privileged few rose to new heights.

> Pierre Goubert, 'The French Peasantry of the Seventeenth Century: A Regional Example', in *Crisis in Europe 1560–1660*, ed. Trevor Aston (London, Routledge & Kegan Paul, 5th imp., 1975), pp 164–5

Questions

a From your knowledge of the reign, explain and comment on (i) 'the drastic reorganisation of the *seigneuries* held by the bourgeoisie and clergy' (lines 22–3); (ii) 'The condition of the peasantry under Louis XIV is, in fact, the product of an exceptional convergence of unfavourable factors' (lines 26–7); (iii) 'This time, too, the great abbeys took part in the kill' (lines 41–2); (iv) 'the powerful caste of the big *fermiers-receveurs*' (line 45).

b Explain, from the passage as a whole, Goubert's claim in the last sentence.

c Suggest why the 'catastrophic increases in prices and poverty' (line 37) round 1694 and 1710 'led to yet another transfer of thousands of acres of plough-land to the bourgeoisie' (lines 38–9).

IV Great Deeds Achieved

Introduction

Any attempt to assess the achievements of Louis XIV during the years 1667–84 poses two sets of important questions. In the first place, how much credit should the king be given? To what extent (if any) can it be said that both the War of Devolution and the Dutch War were the realisation of his long-matured plans? '[I]f Louis had a grand design or long-range program for his policy,' writes J. B. Wolf, 'he failed to leave us its blueprint.' What Helmut Bohme has recently suggested about the study of Bismarck may apply perhaps with equal vigour to any sane approach to Louis XIV's real achievements: 'to look to right and left of the hero figure; to turn one's attention . . . to the *conditions* in which his individual policy was conducted.' In evaluating the relationship between Louis and his 'great deeds', one should therefore take into account such considerations as the true strength of France bequeathed by Richelieu and Mazarin, the relative weakness of the rest of Europe, the psychological impact of the Ottoman threat to the Empire, expert military advice, economic factors, contemporary monarchical conventions, the impoverished populace 'bled white' by taxation and the occasional fortuitous turn in the course of events. To underestimate the value of each of these forces which conditioned Louis XIV's 'grand design' is to ascribe to the view of the Sun King propagated by Boileau and Racine, his Historiographers Royal, and the conventional praise they so abundantly lavished on him.

In the second place, to fail to identify the errors of judgement which marked precisely the realisation of Louis XIV's highest aspirations of grandeur and glory is to distort the true image of the king. The War of Devolution shattered the traditional Bourbon alliance with the United Provinces. 'The Dutch, who had always been eager to have the French as friends,' after the conquest of Franche-Comté 'trembled at the thought of having them as neighbours' (Voltaire). How wise was Louis to react so aggressively to this 'ingratitude'? 'The general war which followed,' claims Briggs, 'brought an end to most of Colbert's reforms, while the peace settlement at Nijmegen in 1679 gave France border territories which could have been much more cheaply won.' His military triumphs during these years were marred by inherent flaws which generally pass unnoticed to the complacent admirer. The policy of the *réunions*, which annexed to France the four great fortresses of Lille, Besançon, Strasburg and Luxembourg, underscored one other aspect of Louis XIV, now officially declared *le grand* and superbly depicted as a god by Le Brun on the vaults at Versailles. Not only were his weaknesses 'never redressed'. They were further 'aggravated by an excessive pride' which dominated his personality (Zeller). ' In reaching far too much,' Louis 'laid the foundations for his own setbacks' (Ranum).

Awareness of these 'errors', however, should not be allowed to blot out of one's view the brilliance of Louis XIV's diplomatic achievements. His foreign policy, says André Latreille, 'aspired to well-chosen annexations, sufficiently justified by geographic and human conditions totally to enter the national heritage. It was rarely misled into chimeras.' Only through a balanced view can one hope to arrive at the true perspective.

By 1684 Louis XIV had reached 'the highest level of his reign' and had almost become the sole arbiter of Europe. 'He owed it to his army, but also to his diplomacy, which was pre-eminent. He owed it, too, to the intellectual superiority of France at the time, and to the perfection which the language reached just then' (Acton). The magnificent court had just been established at Versailles.

1 Sébastien Vauban

Monsieur de Vauban, having personally directed fifty sieges during the reign of Louis the Great, was in a better position than anyone else to set down his reflections on the art of attack and defence; to set right that which he had claimed to be defective in the prevailing
5 concept of fortification, as well as to discuss the best manner of approaching a fortress, attacking it and conquering it; in a word, to lay down sure rules for besieger and besieged, to conduct with art and wisdom their actions and manoeuvres, and to oppose a stubborn and formidable defence and mount the most vigorous and well
10 concerted attack.

> From the Editor's Preface to *De l'Attaque et de la Defence des Places: Par M. de Vauban, Maréchal de France & Directeur Général des Fortifications du Royame* (The Hague, Pierre de Hondt, 1737)

Questions

a What, according to this extract, are the reasons for Vauban's claim to fame? How far, do you think, are they justified?

* c

b   Explain the historical significance of 'the prevailing concept of fortification' (lines 4–5) and comment briefly on what Vauban claimed to have found 'defective' in it.

c   'The work of Vauban in the years of victory saved France in the years of defeat' (Treasure). In the light of this quotation, discuss briefly Vauban's contribution to the military glory of France under Louis XIV.

2   Boileau: 'What Lies Ahead Of Us?'

I understand all is to be subdued:
We'll cross the boundless Libyan sands,
Bring under our control Egyptian and Arabian lands,
Obtain the shores where flows the Ganges toward the East,
5   Lay down the Scythians camped the Pontus bank along,
Thus bringing endless tracts beneath our sway.
But those great deeds achieved, what lies ahead of us?
– Oh then, dear friend, oh then, victorious, satisfied,
Our mind released from care, we'll lead a merry life . . .
10   – From this time on, great King, here in your castle,
Enjoy in peace your days from morn till night!

Widespread the fame of those renowned in siege and battle,
While those who sacrifice for peace – they go unsung.
The names of conquerors, sword in hand, are legion,
15   Each cent'ry boasts its own.
Yet are there not more worthy deeds
Than those of warring heroes?

How rare are kings intent on peace
And subjects' happiness! How rare are they!
20   A search through score on score of years
Yields scarce a name.

> Nicolas Boileau, *Oeuvres*, ed. Berriat Saint-Prix (1830), vol ii, 'Epitre I', p 13

Questions

a   Who was Boileau?

b   What ideal is Boileau trying to express to Louis XIV?

c   It has been claimed that by his Satires, 'Boileau hoped to give support to Colbert'. Suggest how, using this poem to illustrate your answer.

d   Discuss briefly the imagery Boileau uses in the first eleven lines. How far and for what reasons, do you think, is it historically apt?

3 The War of Devolution

(a) The king's view

The death of the king of Spain and the war of the English against the Dutch offered me at once two important occasions for making war: one against Spain for the pursuance of rights which had fallen to me; the other against England for the defence of the Dutch. I saw with
5 pleasure the plan of these two wars as a vast field where great occasions might arise for distinguishing myself. Many brave men whom I saw devoted to my service seemed always to be begging me to offer them an opportunity for valour. . . . Moreover, since I was obliged in any case to maintain a large army, it was more expedient
10 for me to throw it into the Low Countries than to feed it at my expense. . . . Under pretext of a war with England I would dispose of my forces and my information service to begin more successfully my enterprise in Holland.

A *Mémoire* by Louis XIV, in his *Mémoires . . . Réflexions . . .*
Instructions (Paris, 1923), pp 122–5

(b) A historian's view

Europe, divided between fear and favour, saw with astonishment
15 Louis XIV take the field in the month of May, 1667. 'It is not,' said the manifesto sent by the king to the court of Spain, 'either the ambition of possessing new States or the desire of winning glory by arms which inspires the Most Christian King with the design of maintaining the rights of the queen his wife; but would it not be
20 shame for a king to allow all the privileges of blood and of law to be violated in the persons of himself, his wife and his son? As king, he feels himself obliged to prevent this injustice; as master, to oppose this usurpation; and, as father, to secure the patrimony of his son. He has no desire to employ force to open the gates, but he wishes to
25 enter as a beneficent sun by the rays of his love, and to scatter everywhere in country, towns and private houses the gentle influences of abundance and peace which follow in his train.' To secure the *gentle influences of peace*, Louis XIV had collected an army of fifty thousand men, carefully armed and equipped under the
30 supervision of Turenne, to whom Louvois as yet rendered docile obedience. . . . 'Heaven not having ordained any tribunal on earth at which the Kings of France can demand justice, the Most Christian King has only his own arms to look to for it,' said the manifesto. . . .
35 The Spaniards were taken unprepared: Armentières, Charleroi, Douai and Tournay . . . fell almost without striking a blow. Whilst the army was busy with the siege of Courtray, Louis XIV returned to Compiègne to fetch the queen. The whole court followed him to the camp. 'All that you have read about the magnificence of

40   Solomon and the grandeur of the king of Persia, is not to be
compared with the pomp that attends the king in his expedition,'
says a letter to Bussy-Rabutin from the count of Cologny. 'You see
passing along the streets nothing but plumes, gold-laced uniforms,
chariots, mules superbly harnessed, parade-horses, housings with
45   embroidery of fine gold.'

> F. P. G. Guizot, *The History of France from the Earliest Times to
> the Year 1789*, trans R. Black, vol iv (London, 1881),
> pp 293–4

Questions

a   Explain and comment briefly on the historical background of (i)
the 'rights which had fallen to me' (line 3); (ii) 'my information
service' (line 12).

b   What, according to extract *a*, were Louis XIV's motives for the
War of Devolution? Does your wider knowledge of his reign
suggest that he had *other* motives?

c   Identify 'the manifesto sent by the king to the court of Spain' (line
16). This manifesto put up 'a facade of legalism', behind which
'his actions were those of military necessity' (Treasure). How
does extract *b* bear out this judgement?

d   Who was (i) Turenne (line 30); (ii) Louvois (line 30); (iii)
Bussy-Rabutin (line 42)?

e   'Louis XIV's first campaign had been nothing but playing at
war, almost entirely without danger or bloodshed; it had,
nevertheless, been sufficient to alarm Europe' (Guizot). How did
Europe react?

f   In May 1668 the treaty of Aix-la-Chapelle between France and
Spain brought the war to an end. By this time, 'the Queen's
rights remained to be decided'. What, then, had compelled Louis
to end the war?

g   As a French statesman, deeply involved in nineteenth-century
French politics, Guizot used history 'not as an object of serious
study but as a pretext for the expression of his own dogmatisms'
(Anderson). What 'prejudices', do you think, can be discerned in
his extract? From your knowledge of the period, do you consider
his view of the war a balanced one?

4   Racine on the Origins of the Dutch War

The United Netherlands . . . carried the commerce to the Indies
where it almost destroyed the power of Portugal; it treated as an
equal with England . . . whose vessels it burned in the Thames. . . .
Blinded by prosperity it failed to recognise the hand that so many
5   times strengthened and supported it. Leagued with the enemies of
France, it pretended to give law to Europe, and prided itself on

limiting the conquests of the King. It oppressed Catholics . . . it
opposed French commerce in the East. In a word, it failed at nothing
that could bring down a storm that would inundate it. . . . The
10 King, tired of these insolences, resolved to punish them. He declared
war on the Dutch . . . and marched against them. The vigour of his
march astonished them. However criminal they were, they did not
believe that punishment would follow so swiftly. . . . They could
hardly believe that a young prince, born with all the graces of body
15 and mind . . . in the midst of pleasures . . . would be able so easily
. . . to go far from his kingdom, and to expose himself to the fatigues
of a long and troublesome war with uncertainty of its success.

Jean Racine, *La précise historique des campagnes de Louis Le
Grand*, quoted in Wolf, op cit, p 633, notes 4, 5

Questions

a Are the 'insolences' which Racine mentions in the first eight lines
justifiable?
b From your knowledge of his reign, what, do you think, were
Louis' real aims when he 'declared war on the Dutch'? Were they
accomplished?
c How reliable do you consider Racine's views on the origins of the
Dutch war to be as a historical source? How important are they?

5 Zuane Moresini, Venetian Ambassador in France, to the Doge & Senate, 27 August 1670

The Spanish ambassador has been to see me at this house, and took
the occasion to express his fears and apprehensions of the invasion of
the Spanish possessions in Flanders. The most considerable matter
that I have succeeded in discovering and which I recognise to be
5 worthy of the state's knowledge is the result of numerous
conferences between the king, the ministers and the duke of
Buckingham, the British envoy. Many of the articles and
conclusions ventilated have reached my ears and I think it my duty to
give your Excellencies an account.
10 Buckingham has been urged by the king here to persuade the
British king on his return to contract an ever increasing union and
confidence with this side, to the detriment of Holland. . . . [The
Duke] intimated that before his Britannic Majesty can consent to the
declarations which are desired here, he believed that it would be
15 necessary to decide to establish considerable advantages in trade for
England on both sides of the line, without which it would not be
possible for them to consent to any negotiation or business. If the
British king should receive from France advantages equal to those
which he at present enjoys as chief in the triple alliance, he would,

20 without hesitation, prefer confidential relations with this kingdom
to those which he now cherishes with the States of Holland.
  The memory of the insults inflicted by the United Provinces upon
the royal dignity and upon their arms was deeply engraved on the
hearts of everyone in England. The British king would use for his
25 own advantage the very serious difficulties in which the States now
find themselves, in which he recognises that he is not able alone to
destroy their vigour and power. That king has a peculiar regard
personally for his Most Christian Majesty combined with affection
and intimacy, and if it were left to him alone he would overcome the
30 various difficulties. . . . Nevertheless Buckingham pointed out as a
great obstacle the very careful estimate made by order of the British
king of the number of vessels which constitute the universal
commerce of Europe. This amounts to some 24,000, of which over
16,000 are in the power and at the free disposition of the Dutch. The
35 United Provinces ought in any case to feel the pinch first of all at sea
as in their possessions on land they were strongly protected against
losses by numerous strong places, all of them considerable.
  Before entering upon the proposed rupture with the States various
measures are necessary between the two kingdoms for the purpose
40 of removing the jealousies and misgivings of their neighbours and to
reassure the Catholic Court about the intentions of the two crowns
of France and England. The question was a serious one in itself and
the consequences most weighty. . . .
  With the personal animosity of the king against the States of
45 Holland, with the ill feeling which persists and is constantly
increasing between this crown and the United Provinces it will
prove, in my opinion, an exceedingly difficult matter for ministers
to restrain the course of some royal enterprise against these same
States. The thing that seems at present quite inevitable is a naval
50 union between France and England to the detriment of the
Dutch. . . .This may possibly be followed up, at an opportune
moment, by an attack on the States by land if they are able to find
some means calculated to allay the apprehensions and misgivings of
the Spaniards and the other neighbouring powers.
55 None the less this grave project is bound up with numerous
difficulties and possible variations.

Calendar of State Papers (Venetian), ed. A. B. Hinds, vol xxxvi
(1669–70) (London, H.M.S.O., 1937), pp 256–8

Questions

a Identify (i) Buckingham (line 10); (ii) 'the triple alliance' (line 19);
(iii) 'the very serious difficulties in which the States now find
themselves' (lines 25–6).
b What, do you think, does Moresini mean by the 'advantages' the
British king 'at present enjoys as chief in the triple alliance' (line
19)?

c Why, according to Moresini's account, should the British king 'prefer confidential relations' with France 'to those which he now cherishes with the States of Holland' (lines 20–21)?

d '[I]f it were left to him alone' (line 29). What does the author mean by this?

e Explain and comment briefly on the historical background to lines 38–43.

f How accurate or otherwise has Moresini's judgement in lines 55–6 been proved by subsequent events?

6 Reports of Political Imbroglios?

(a) Girolamo Alberti, Venetian Secretary in England, to the Doge & Senate, London, 6 March 1671

Last week I wrote of the suspicions and resolves of England. I have since urged a person of great credit at Court to get more definite information through confidential intercourse with the ministers. As he and all his family have always professed great regard for the
5 republic he was glad to be able to reveal the secret to me. It confirms what I have always intimated, that this Court is less allied with France than is supposed from appearances, and no secret treaty exists, as England is aware of the advantage of enjoying quiet by maintaining the alliance. To retain control over the powers of which
10 it is composed she did not rush into pledges with them, suspecting that, being considered colleagues in danger, they would not be deemed the champions of the common weal and of liberty. If Sweden stands fast and Holland resists the temptations and forces of the Most Christian king, then measures will be taken, if necessary;
15 but if any of the parties concerned change their colours and disturb the conditions of the peace, England can always be in time to enlist herself on one side or the other and by not placing too much trust in either, risk nothing. This is the foundation on which all the negotiations turn.
20 I may add that there is a strong suspicion that all the preparations of the Most Christian, which from so many indications seem directed against Holland, relate to other undertakings, it being his custom to make countermarches, and on principle he disapproves of showing himself in arms against a power so long before attacking it.

Calendar of State Papers (Venetian), op cit, vol xxxvii (1671–2) pp 23–4

(b) Girolamo Alberti, Venetian Secretary in England, to the Doge & Senate, London, 3 June 1672

25 Not until late did the Dutch become aware of the time they had lost and the friends they had neglected. They deceived themselves with

the notion that his Britannic Majesty was unable to wage war on them and would not choose to join France. Had this not been the case they would have sacrificed considerable sums for peace, and they repented their mistake in not purchasing confidential allies. This mistake is irremediable and in their distress the Dutch have recourse to feeble counsel. Carried away by passion their satirical effusions are redoubled and they excite rebellion against the king of England, as if they could never again expect peace, whereas by exasperating his Majesty they could not fail to draw upon themselves a more protracted and disastrous war.

The English ministers in fact consider that they possess the keys of peace and war. Lord Arlington told me formally that the Dutch had allowed themselves to be carried away to the last paroxysm of rage, giving way to malicious disrespect towards a great king and descending to satire, a manner of revenge unworthy even of private individuals, and endeavouring through the press to raise rebellion, weapons peculiar to civil war alone. One of the internal motives of the war was the unbearable effrontery of the Dutch, who fancy themselves established in possession of the revolted provinces and at liberty to abuse all sovereigns. Not satisfied with this and growing daily worse they have now represented his Britannic Majesty with a ring through his nose led by the king of France. They formerly depicted the king of England and the United Provinces dancing on a tight rope with the Most Christian king playing the fiddle below, and the legend, 'The first who falls will pay the fiddler.' After this they composed a most scurrilous libel in the Flemish tongue, of which the English had no need, being already too turbulent. . . .

If not actually dangerous the unguarded manner with which the Spanish ambassador at this Court speaks is very unpalatable and little by little he is losing their confidence. Now that the Spaniards are recovering from the agony of their surprise by the Most Christian they are beginning to take breath. . . .

Your Serenity will have heard from elsewhere how at Lisbon the treaty for an alliance with the king there is advancing. It appears that Melo, the Portuguese ambassador here, writes warmly to induce him to join the allied crowns, so as to prevent Spain from making any stir in favour of Holland. I have just been told that the Most Christian has sent 500,000 livres to England for the cost of the present armament.

Ibid, pp 221–2

Questions

a Identify (i) 'the republic' (lines 4–5); (ii) 'the powers of which [the alliance] is composed' (lines 9–10); (iii) Lord Arlington (line 38).
b From your historical knowledge, what do you understand by 'being considered colleagues in danger' (line 11)? Explain Alberti's reference to British 'suspicions' in lines 10–12.

c   What evidence could Alberti have had by March 1671 in support
      of his claim in lines 22–4?

d   Explain the historical significance of (i) the first sentence of
      extract *b* (ii) the reference to the Spaniards in lines 56–8.

e   Explain and comment briefly on (i) the historical significance of
      lines 46–51 (ii) the importance of anonymous 'scurrilous'
      pamphlet literature to the historian.

f   How reliable are accounts such as Alberti's and Moresini's
      (document 5) as historical evidence? Explain fully why.

7   The Siege of Bouchain, 11 May 1676

The King was easily aroused from his sleep [by von Schomberg]. He
immediately mounted his horse and set out for Heurtevise, which
was only a cannon-shot from Valenciennes, followed by only eight
squadrons of the guards, four of his gendarmes, and his light horse.
5   His Majesty, on seeing thirteen squadrons in battle formation under
the counter-escarpment of Valenciennes, thought at first that it was
the garrison cavalry. He saw a moment later that the enemy formed
an extended cavalry wing. Wishing to take advantage of the
moment, and not to give them time to be reinforced by a larger
10 corps, the King proposed to charge them, but, knowing by the
respectful silence, and then, by the opinion of the most experienced
officers . . . when he ordered them to express [it], that the difference
in the [enemy] number – which increased every moment – as well as
the decisive advantage of the enemy position, would mean that such
15 an order would not be followed by happy success. He [thus] decided
to await the arrival of the troops, while remaining with the small
number that accompanied him in the presence of his enemies, whose
battalions extended to the woods and whose squadrons formed a
second line. The word reached the army that . . . the King with
20 several squadrons was within cannon-shot of Valenciennes and the
enemy in line of battle. . . .
   The King, with an unbelievable coolness, placed his army in battle
formation as it arrived, extending his right near to Valenciennes and
his left up to the woods of Saint Armand. Nothing escaped his
25 Majesty's skill and foresight. . . . The general officers took their
places after all his orders had been given and executed in short
without confusion. . . . [Then] the King ordered the firing of three
cannon shots to tell the enemy of the desire and the intention that he
had to give battle and to assure them that he waited and sought the
30 opportunity. . . .
   The day passed with several slight skirmishes. The Marshal
d'Humières returned to join the army with his detachment; Marshal
de Créqui returned in the evening to his camp before Bouchain;
Monsieur went there also the next day . . . and began the assault in

35 full daylight. . . . The fortification surrendered, and the enemy was
    informed by three discharges of cannon fire.

Extract from the Marquis de Louvois' official account of the
siege, quoted in Wolf, op cit, pp 250–1

Questions

a   Identify (i) Marshal d'Humières (lines 31–2); (ii) Marshal de
    Créqui (lines 32–3); (iii) Monsieur (line 34).
b   Discuss briefly Wolf's view that the siege of Bouchain 'turned
    out to be the only opportunity that Louis ever had to win a
    military reputation, but the chance slipped from his grasp'.
c   From your knowledge of the king's character, do you agree with
    Saint-Simon that this occasion showed Louis' cowardice and fear
    of battle?
d   Suggest reasons why Louvois fails to explain the 'critical
    decision' why Louis did not fall on the enemy 'when the
    opportunity presented itself several days before, and winning a
    decisive victory'.
e   'Yet,' claims Voltaire, 'the glory of the field remained with the
    king, since he achieved what he wished to do and took a town in
    the face of the enemy.' Comment briefly on this view.
f   What positive feature of Louis' character does Louvois' account
    reveal?
g   What importance do official accounts such as Louvois' have as
    historical sources?

8   Nijmegen, 10 August 1678: Apex of Power and Glory

[The peace] terms were laid down with the arrogance of a conqueror;
nevertheless they were not so outrageous as to render his enemies
desperate and force them to reunite against him in a final effort: he
spoke to Europe as a master, but at the same time acted as a
5   statesman. . . .
    None of the conditions laid down by Louis XIV was altered. His
enemies would have bluffed in vain had they submitted better terms
to cloak their weakness: Europe received not only laws but peace
from Louis. The Duke of Lorraine alone dared to refuse a treaty
10 which seemed to him too odious; preferring to be a wandering
prince within the Empire than a sovereign with neither power nor
dignity in his own estates; he trusted to time and courage to restore
his fortunes. . . . This peace is a good example of how
contradictory are the designs of men and their subsequent results.
15 Holland, against whom alone the war had been waged and who
should have been ruined, lost nothing; indeed she gained a barrier; all

the other powers who had guaranteed her from annihilation lost something.

The king was at this time at the height of his greatness. Victorious
20 since he had begun to reign, having besieged no place which he had not taken, superior in every way to his united enemies, for six years the terror of Europe and at last her arbitrator and peacemaker, he now added Franche-Comté, Dunkirk and half Flanders to his possessions; moreover, and he might well count this the greatest of
25 his advantages, he was the king of a nation happy in itself and the model of all others.

Some time afterwards, in 1680, the Council of Paris conferred the title of *Great* upon him.

Voltaire, op cit, pp 124–6

Questions

a   From your knowledge of this period, do you agree with Voltaire that the terms of the peace treaty of Nijmegen were not 'outrageous' (line 2)? Explain fully why.

b   In what way may Louis be said to have 'acted as a statesman' in 1678?

c   What do you understand by 'Europe received not only laws but peace from Louis' (lines 8–9)?

d   Explain and comment briefly on the historical significance of Voltaire's remarks in lines 15–18.

★ e   From your knowledge of Louis XIV's reign, how valid, do you think, is Voltaire's description of France in 1678 as 'a nation happy in itself and the model of all others' (lines 25–6)?

f   'For the time Louis had a clear field; his future would depend upon the way he interpreted Nijmegen' (Treasure). Discuss this statement briefly in the light of Voltaire's extract.

V   Church–State Relations

Introduction

The assertive posture which the young king assumed towards the papacy over Créqui's mission to Rome in 1662 marked the aggressive tone of his future relations with the Holy See. Louis' truculent attitude towards ecclesiastical policies would eventually involve him into 'grave errors of judgement with far-reaching consequences' (Stoye). The *régale* dispute was typical. How far was it the natural outcome of his 'new conception of the State' and 'exaggerated idea of sovereignty' (Immich)? How genuine was his desire to impose uniformity throughout his realm? Or was the extension of the *régale*, rather, a wise Colbertian economic expedient? From an 'apparently trivial' issue, it soon turned into an 'immeasurably' serious conflict with the resolute Innocent XI, which revived 'all the ancient emotions about Gallican liberties' (Pennington). Why could not the civil authority exempt itself of its obligation to abide by the decisions of the Catholic Church in matters not entirely theological (Philippson)? This claim, supported by the complacent 'seminarian pedants' (Saint-Simon) and the widely influential Jesuits, led unequivocally to the 'radical manifesto' of the Gallican Faith. The dispute dragged on till 1693.

If the king's inordinate zeal for *gloire* would not tolerate any foreign interference within his realm, still less would his pathological obsession with the divine purpose of his kingship allow 'room for dissent'. Protestantism constituted the first threat to his ideal of national unity. By the Edict of Fontainebleau, the 'new Constantine' tried to eliminate the Huguenots from France completely. The Edict was publicly acclaimed as a 'miracle' by Bossuet and secretly denounced as unnecessary and sacrilegious by Saint-Simon. But how creditable are such views? To assess the true consequences of the Revocation, certain problems need to be reconsidered in the light of recent research. In what ways (if any), and to what extent, did it 'weaken' France and 'strengthen' her enemies? How far should we really believe the evidence of eye-witnesses' reports?

The second threat came from Jansenism. Urged on by Louis himself in an attempt to curb its widespread influence, Clement XI condemned the movement in two bulls, the *Vineam Domini* (1705) and the *Unigenitus Dei* (1713). The latter was highly controversial. Meant 'to prevent a schism', the *Unigenitus* 'was near to causing one' (Voltaire). It was only through the otherwise ailing strength of the monarch that Archbishop Noailles, the *Parlement* and the Sorbonne were ultimately forced to yield. This gives rise to important questions: did not Louis XIV's 'resort to personal intimidation' destroy 'the working alliance he had always sought to maintain with his clergy'? On the other hand, did it not 'paradoxically' identify 'church and state more closely than ever since Louis had thus made himself the sole arbiter in a theological dispute' (Maland)? Finally, how can one explain Louis XIV's transformation from 'the most uncompromising defender of Gallicanism' into 'the advocate of ultramontanism' (Lockyer)?

While disputes raged over the Huguenots and the Jansenists, there emerged yet another threat to orthodoxy in the form of the mystical Quietist religion, which involved the two outstanding theological geniuses – Bossuet and Fénelon – into one of the worst complicated disputes over the spiritual claims of a Madame Guyon.

'Louis XIV regarded his religious policy as the most important element of his rule; he did not succeed in it' (Lavisse). This raises the issue of how far Louis' decisions were influenced by the men (and women) around him. How much personal responsibility should be attached to him for the imposition and ultimate failure of religious uniformity?

1   The stage is set

I must not conceal the fact, that if the imprudent pride of the Chigi family has caused them to fall into the ditch, their ambitious blundering has miserably entangled them in it. These people persuaded themselves that Rome was the world; but the king of
5   France has given them to know, and that at their own cost, that they had not studied geography well. Much gossiping has caused the general feeling to be pretty well known in respect of the insolence of Cardinal [Lorenzo] Imperiali and Don Mario [Chigi, the Pope's brother] concerning the immunities of the French ambassador. I will
10 not say that they were blameless, but . . . to their ill-will there was conjoined some fault of chance, which not unfrequently diminishes or increases the effect of human labours. This it is in part which has constituted their guilt, and now compels them to make full satisfaction to such claims as the king of France may legitimately
15 found on the affronts that he has too certainly received in the person of his ambassador. But since I know the truth of this matter, so did I use indefatigable efforts to cool down the rage of Créqui, and apply the balsams of negotiation to this schism, before it had extended to

what was manifest ruin. But there were too many fancies in the
20   heads of those Chigis, and too much obstinacy, to permit their
condescending to a suitable humiliation towards the king, whose
bravados they would not believe, considering them a mere pretence,
. . . a little ephemeral French heat. And this went so far, that his
holiness told me the Roman hearts were not to be frightened by the
25   rhodomontade of a French stripling. To which I replied, that it was
sometimes more dangerous to have to do with hare-brained boys
than with older and wiser heads . . .; moreover, that to play with
those who, if they have whims in their heads, have also armies at
their sides, and millions under their feet, was not a fit game for the
30   popes, who have nothing but their two raised fingers. . . . But all
these, and a hundred other powerful reasons, were equally vain, he
having too much affection for his kindred to send them away, and
being, besides, too much displeased about the matter of Castro. . . .
One day . . . he said to me . . .: 'Every one cries out that Castro
35   must be given up, but no one says that Avignon ought to be restored;
every one declares that the king must receive satisfaction for the
affronts offered him, but no one utters a word of the compensation
that should be made to ecclesiastics for the injuries they have
endured.'

> Report from Rome, by the Venetian Cardinal Pietro
> Basadona, Archbishop of Aix, 1663, in L. Ranke, *History of
> the Popes*, trans. by E. Foster, vol iii, (London, 1856),
> pp 436–7

Questions

a   Identify (i) the Chigi family (lines 1–2); (ii) Créqui (line 17).
b   Explain the reference to (i) 'some fault of chance' (line 11); (ii) 'the
matter of Castro' (line 33); (iii) Avignon (line 35).
c   Suggest what Basadona means when he says 'to play . . . fingers'
in lines 27–30.
d   What exactly were Louis' claims for satisfaction (lines 14–16)?
★ e   The Pope had grossly underestimated the young king. Explain
how events proved the wisdom of Pietro Basadona's advice in
lines 25–30.
★ f   Comment on the view that Louis XIV's 'willingness to join in a
crusade against the Turks' in 1664 was meant 'to attentuate the
painful impression' which his action towards the Pope in 1662
had created 'in the Catholic world' (Pastor).

2   The Jesuits

(a) Paris, February 25, 1656. Sir, Nothing can come up to the Jesuits.
I have seen Jacobins, doctors, and all sorts of people in my day, but
such an interview as I have just had was wanting to complete my

knowledge of mankind. Other men are merely copies of them. As
things are always found best at the fountainhead, I paid a visit to one
of the ablest among them, in company with my trusty
Jansenist. . . . Being particularly anxious to learn something of a
dispute which they have with the Jansenists about what they call
actual grace, I said to the worthy father that I would be much obliged
to him if he would instruct me on this point – that I did not even
know what the term meant and would thank him to explain it. 'With
all my heart,' the Jesuit replied; 'for I dearly love inquisitive people.
Actual grace, according to our definition, is an inspiration of God,
whereby He makes us to know His will and excites within us a desire
to perform it.'

'And where,' said I, 'lies your difference with the Jansenists on this
subject?'

'The difference lies here,' he replied; 'we hold that God bestows
actual grace *on all men in every case of temptation*; for we maintain that
unless a person have, whenever tempted, actual grace to keep him
from sinning, his sin, whatever it may be, can never be imputed to
him. The Jansenists, on the other hand, affirm that sins, though
committed without actual grace, are, nevertheless, imputed; but
they are a pack of fools.' . . .

Astonished at such a declaration, according to which, no sins of
surprise, nor any of those committed in entire forgetfulness of God,
could be imputed, I turned round to my friend the Jansenist and
easily discovered from his looks that he was of a different way of
thinking.

(b) To Father Annat, Jesuit. January 23, 1657. . . . Reverend
Father, if you have found any difficulty in deciphering this letter,
which is certainly not printed in the best possible type, blame
nobody but yourself. Privileges are not so easily granted to me as
they are to you. You can procure them even for the purpose of
combating miracles; I cannot have them even to defend myself. The
printing-houses are perpetually haunted. In such circumstances, you
yourself would not advise me to write you any more letters, for it is
really a sad annoyance to be obliged to have recourse to an
Osnabruck impression.

> Blaise Pascal, *The Provincial Letters*, trans. by T. M'Crie in
> *Great Books of the Western World*, ed. by R. Maynard
> Hutchins, vol 33, *Pascal* (Chicago, 1952), extracts from
> Letter IV, pp 19–20 and Letter XVII, p 153

Questions

a   What is Pascal's attitude towards the Jesuits? Does the impression
he creates of them in the two extracts conform to your views?

   b Do you think that the 'dispute' between the Jesuits and the Jansenists was *simply* over the doctrine of *actual grace*? Explain fully.

   c What features of Pascal's style are evident in both extracts?

   d Explain the historical significance of extract *b*.

★   *e* From your knowledge of the period, how influential, do you feel, were the Jesuits (i) in French society (ii) on Louis' religious policy?

3 The Four Gallican Articles 19 March 1682

We, the archbishops and bishops gathered in Paris by Royal command, representing the Gallican Church, together with other churchmen . . . have decided that the following articles should be promulgated and declared:

5 1. Power has been conferred by God on blessed Peter and his successors, Vicars of Christ Himself, a power over the spiritual things of the Church and those which pertain to eternal salvation, but not over civil and temporal matters. . . . Consequently kings and princes are not subjected by the ordinance of God to any

10 ecclesiastical authority in temporal affairs; nor by the authority of the keys of the Church can they be deposed, directly or indirectly, nor can their subjects be dispensed from loyalty and obedience or absolved from the oath of fidelity which they have taken. This judgement is to be universally held as necessary to public quietness,

15 useful to the Church as well as to secular authority and agreeable to the word of God, the tradition of the fathers, and the examples of the Saints.

2. Full authority in spiritual matters is, however, inherent in the Apostolic See and the successors of Peter the Vicar of Christ, while at

20 the same time the decrees of the Holy General Council of Constance . . . concerning the authority of General Councils, are to remain valid and unchanged, approved, as they are, by the Apostolic See and by the practice of the Roman Pontiffs themselves and of the whole Church; nor may the Gallican Church give approval to those

25 who minimise the force of those decrees, as if they were of doubtful authority and little backing, or who disparage the statements of the Council as referring only to the time of schism.

3. Hence the exercise of the Apostolic authority should be moderated by the Canons established by the Holy Spirit and

30 consecrated by the respect of the whole world. Also the rules, customs and institutions accepted in the French kingdom and Church are to keep their force and the bounds fixed by our fathers are to remain undisturbed; for it is essential for the dignity of the Apostolic See, that statutes and customs, confirmed by the consent

35 of that See itself and of the churches, should enjoy their rightful
    stability.
    4. In questions of faith the leading role is to be that of the Supreme
    Pontiff; and his decrees apply to all churches in general and to each of
    them in particular. But his judgement is not unchangeable, unless it
40 receives the consent of the Church.

> H. L. Lear, *Bossuet and His Contemporaries* (Rivingtons,
> 1874), pp 265–6

Questions

a Explain the reference to (i) 'the decrees . . . Constance' in line 20;
  (ii) 'the time of schism' (line 27).

★ b Analyse carefully the circumstances leading to the Gallican
  Declaration.

c Comment on the significance of each of the four Articles in an
  attempt to arrive at a definition of Gallicanism.

★ d Suggest why the cause of Gallicanism, based essentially on
  medieval principles and ideas, was revived and gained headway
  again during *le grande siècle*.

4 Gallican Bishops' Apology to Innocent XII 14 September 1693

Nothing grieves me so much as the fact that whilst the Church
flourishes so happily, my own situation seems to have excluded me
in some way from the favour of your Holiness' predecessors. Hence
I declare that all that may be considered as having been decided in
5   that Assembly concerning the power of the Church and the
authority of the Pope, I consider as not decided and as not to be
decided. Furthermore I hold as not determined all that might be
considered as having been determined to the detriment of the rights
of the Church; on the contrary I declare myself ready for the most
10 complete submission to your Holiness. For it was never my
intention to do anything detrimental to the Church, on the contrary,
I protest my sincerest submission to your Holiness.

> Quoted in L. F. von Pastor, *The History of the Popes from the
> close of the Middle Ages*, vol xxxii (London, 1957), trans. by
> D. E. Graff, p 600

Questions

a Explain the distress expressed by the bishops in the first sentence
  over their 'own situation'.

b What altered circumstances had forced Louis XIV in 1693 to yield
  to the Papacy?

★ c 'Louis did not go to Canossa, but he made his pliant Bishops take
  that road.' Comment on this view.

5 Bossuet's Attack upon Protestantism

The Reformation was founded upon the notion that one may
re-examine all decisions of the Church, and judge them in light of
Scriptures – because the Church may err in doctrine having no
promise of infallible assistance from the Holy Spirit. Thus its
5   opinions are but human, and there is no authority upon earth capable
of determining the true sense of Scriptures, nor of fixing for all the
dogmas which compose Christianity. Such is the basis, such is the
genius of the Reformation. . . . Almost all of Christianity has been
put in question. The Socinians inundated the Reformation, for it had
10   no barrier with which to oppose them. And in this manner religious
indifference took permanent root. To be convinced of this one need
only listen to Ministre Jurieu. . . . He includes among the Socinians
those who preach tolerance, an immense number of whom are to be
found in the Reformation, and whom he calls the indifferent. . . .
15   'They abused,' says our Ministre, 'the civil toleration then granted
different sects (in Holland) . . .'. But this *civil toleration* . . . goes
much further than one thinks, for, according to Ministre Jurieu,
those who establish it 'have nothing less in mind than the ruin of the
true principles of Christianity . . . to make everything indifferent,
20   and to open the gates to libertinism . . .'.

Thus civil toleration, that is to say, impunity accorded by the
magistrate to all sects, is necessarily associated in the minds of those
who support it with ecclesiastical toleration. If one would declare
openly for ecclesiastical toleration, that is, recognise all heretics as
25   true members and true children of the Church, one would openly
announce his indifference in religious matters. One does the same in
upholding civil toleration. What indeed can it matter to those that
hold religion an indifferent matter that the Church condemn
them? . . . Provided that the magistrate leaves them alone, they
30   enjoy in peace the liberty which they give themselves. . . . This is
why they are so noisy when one excites the magistrate against them:
but their true design is to hide religious indifference under the
bleeding-heart appearance of civil toleration.

> *Oeuvres Completes de Bossuet, Avertissemens aux Protestans sur
> les Lettres du Ministre Jurieu* (Paris, 1862–6), vol xvi, pp 117–
> 24

Questions

a   Identify 'Ministre Jurieu' (line 12) and explain the reference to
    'Socinians' (line 9).
b   Do you find Bossuet's attack on Protestantism as a serious
    political danger tenable? How justified is it in the light of what the
    Huguenots *did* (not what they would have liked to do) before
    1685?

c The revocation of the Edict of Nantes (see next document) confirmed Bossuet's fears of 'civil toleration'. What was his reaction to it?

d Discuss the value of this extract to the historian of the period.

6 Edict of Fontainebleau, October 1685: Preamble

King Henry the Great, our grandfather of glorious memory, desiring to prevent the peace which he had procured for his subjects, after the great losses which they had suffered during the civil and foreign wars, from being disturbed because of the so-called
5 Reformed Religion . . . had – by the Edict given at Nantes in . . . April 1598 – arranged the policy which was to be adopted towards those of the said Religion, the places in which they could practise it, and had established special judges to administer justice for them; finally, he had provided, by specific articles, for everything which he
10 had thought . . . necessary for the maintenance of peace in his kingdom and for the lessening of tension between the two religions, so that he might be in a position to work . . . for the reunion to the Church of those who had so easily removed themselves from it. But the intention of the said king . . . could not be carried out because of
15 his sudden death and as the execution of the aforesaid edict was later interrupted, during the minority of the late king, our . . . father . . ., by their new manoeuvres, the aforesaid followers of the so-called Reformed Religion gave [him] reason . . . to deprive them of several privileges which had been granted to them by the aforesaid edict;
20 nevertheless, the king, our . . . father, displaying his customary clemency, granted them a new edict at Nîmes, in . . . July 1629, by means of which peace having again been established, the said late king, animated with the same spirit and the same zeal for religion as . . . our grandfather, resolved to take advantage of this tranquillity
25 to try to put his pious plan into operation; but, as foreign wars arose a few years afterwards – from 1635 until the truce concluded in 1684 – with the princes of Europe, and the kingdom had had little time free from agitation, it was not possible to do anything for the advancement of religion except to lessen the number of the so-called
30 Reformed Religion's places of worship by the burning of those which were established in contravention of the stipulations of the edicts, and by the suppression of the bipartite courts for whose erection provision had not been made. As God has at last allowed our peoples to enjoy perfect quiet, and as we ourselves are not
35 preoccupied with the cares of protecting them against our enemies, we have been able to profit by this truce which we have facilitated in order to give our whole attention to finding the means to bring to

success the scheme of the aforesaid kings . . . in which we have been engaged since our accession to the Crown.

S. Z. Ehler and J. B. Morrall (eds and trans), *Church and State through the Centuries: A collection of historic documents with commentaries* (London, 1954), pp 209–10

Questions

a Explain the reference to (i) 'the places in which they could practise it' (line 7); (ii) 'new manoeuvres' (line 17); (iii) 'bipartite courts' (line 32); (iv) 'this truce' (line 36).

★ b Compare and contrast the Edict of Nantes and the Edict of Nîmes.

c Comment on the reasons which Louis puts forward in this extract to support his revocation of the Edict of Nantes. How were they received by (i) Louis' contemporary critics (ii) later historians?

d From your knowledge of the period, what part, do you feel, did each of the following play in dictating Louis' decision to revoke the Edict of Nantes: (i) general religious motives; (ii) public opinion; (iii) the international political situation; (iv) his advisers; (v) his 'inordinate desire for *gloire*'?

★ e Discuss the view that in choosing between a 'crusade abroad or one at home' Louis XIV allotted 'to the Huguenots the role that the Turks could no longer play'.

7 Persecution of the Huguenots – An Eye-Witness

3 [November 1685] . . . The French persecution of the Protestants, raging with uttmost barbarity, exceeding what the very heathens used: Innumerable persons of the greatest birth, & riches, leaving all their earthly substance & hardly escaping with their lives, dispers'd
5 thro' all the Countries of Europe: The French Tyrant, abrogating the Edicts of Nants &c in favour of them, & without any Cause on the suddaine, demolishing all their Churches, banishing, Imprisoning, sending to the Gallies all the Ministers: plundring the common people, & exposing them to all sorts of barbarous usage, by souldiers
10 sent to ruine & prey upon them; taking away their children; forcing people to the Masse, & then executing them as Relapsers: They burnt the libraries, pillag'd their goods, eate up their filds and sustenance, banish'd or sent to the Gallies the people, & seiz'd on their Estates: There had now ben numbred to passe through Geneva onely, from
15 time to time by stealth onely (for all the usual passages were strictly guarded by sea and land) fourty thousand, towards Swisserland: In Holland, Denmark, & all about Germany, were dispersed some hundred thousands besids here in England, where though multitude

of all degrees sought for shelter, & wellcome, as distressed
20 Christians & Confessors, they found least encouragement; by a
fatality of the times we were fall'n into, & the incharity &
indifference of such, as should have embrac'd them: . . . The
famous [Jean] Claude fled to Holland: [Pierre] Allix & severall more
came to London: and persons of mighty estates came over who had
25 forsaken all: But France was almost dispeopled, the bankers so
broaken that the Tyrant's revenue exceedingly diminished:
Manufacture ceased, & every body there save the Jesuites &c
abhorring what was don: nor the Papists themselves approving it;
what the intention farther is time will shew, but doubtlesse
30 portending some extraordinary revolution.

> *The Diary of John Evelyn*, ed. by E. S. de Beer (London,
> 1959), pp 832–3

Questions

a Identify (i) Jean Claude (line 23) and (ii) Pierre Allix (line 23).
b Suggest what Evelyn has in mind when he refers to 'a fatality . . .
   embrac'd them' in lines 20–2.
c On what grounds is Evelyn condemning the persecution of the
   French Protestants?
d Which statements in this extract do you consider in need of
   checking? What other sources would you use?
e What contribution does this extract make to your view of the
   draggonades?
* f Were Evelyn's fears, expressed in lines 29–30, of 'some
   extraordinary revolution' borne out by later events?
* g How can this document be used to support the view that the
   'Revocation' diminished 'the strength of France' and increased
   'the strength of her enemies'?
h What value do diaries, which, like Evelyn's, were never
   envisaged for publication, have as historical evidence?

8 Mystical Ardour

(a) Miguel de Molinos

It is necessary that man reduce his own powers to nothingness, and
this is the interior way. . . . By doing nothing the soul annihilates
itself and returns to its beginning and to its origin, which is the
essence of God, in which it remains transformed and divinized, and
5 God then remains in himself, because then the two things are no
more united, but are one alone, and in this manner God lives and
reigns in us, and the soul annihilates itself in operative being.

> Propositions of Molinos, extracted from Innocent XI's Bull
> *Coelestis Pastor*, 20 November 1687, in *Readings in Church
> History*, ed. by C. J. Barry, vol ii (Maryland, 1967), p 275

(b) Mme Guyon

Our surrender then ought to be an entire leaving of ourselves in the
hands of God, both in respect of the outward and inward state,
10 forgetting ourselves in a great measure, and thinking on God only:
by this means the heart remains always free, contented and
disengaged.

> *Moyen court et très facile de faire l'oraison* (1685), trans. by
> D. Macfayden, 1902, p 129

(c) Fénelon, Archbishop of Cambrai

God knows what I do not and that we will either find a new courage
or we will be overwhelmed without being destroyed. God sees in the
15 wealth of His providence the exact means that my feeble reason
cannot uncover. I love what he will do without comprehending it; I
await His decision. He knows with what tenderness I love my
country, with what gratitude and what respectful affection I would
give my life for that of the king, with what zeal and feeling I am
20 attached to the royal house and especially to Monseigneur the Duke
of Burgundy; but I cannot hide my heart: it is due to this strong,
tender, and constant feeling that I wish that our terrible troubles will
bring about the real cure of our political ills so that this violent crisis
will not be without fruit.

> Extract from Fénelon's Letter to the Duc de Chevreuse,
> 4 August 1710, in *Great Lives Observed: Louis XIV*, ed. by
> J. C. Rule (New Jersey, 1974), pp 104–7

Questions

  a What thematic elements do you find in common in these three
     extracts?

★ *b* Comment on the relationship between Molinos, Mme Guyon
     and Fénelon.

  c Suggest what Fénelon has in mind in the last four lines of extract
     c.

★ *d* Why, do you think, was this 'mystical ardour' regarded as a
     threat to orthodoxy and authority and what was the reaction of
     (i) the Church (ii) the State to the movement in France?

9 Clement XI's Letter to Louis XIV, accompanying the Bull *Unigenitus Dei Filius*

We have lately published our Apostolic Constitution on the
notorious French book Reflections on the New Testament, which
our Pastoral office has made necessary and which Your Majesty's
inborn zeal for the faith has even more eagerly called for. Our
5 Venerable Brother Cornelius . . . Papal Nuncio at Your Majesty's

Court will forward it to you on our behalf, and he will more fully explain to Your Majesty that we have not spared any pains or efforts in checking the spread of the plague of this erroneous doctrine within the Catholic Church and especially in your most flourishing
10 Kingdom: so far, the subtler it was, the more harmful it has proved to be. We are struck with extreme wonder and with no less grief by the fact that in one single book, however small in size, so many and such abominably great errors could have possibly found themselves squeezed in, and that with all the art of deception this book is
15 thoroughly undermining both Church and State. It is gradually instilling in the minds of Christian people everywhere, under the attractive guise of piety, hatred and contempt for both ecclesiastical and secular authorities. . . .

In order to achieve our aim more easily and happily, we earnestly ask
20 the kindness of Your Majesty's efficacious help and protection, as we have experienced it on other occasions, and as you yourself have given us ample scope for hoping. On the strength of your assistance we shall eventually succeed in overcoming all the efforts made by the rebels who do not conform to the truth. May this measure of the
25 Apostolic See be received by all with utmost reverence and observed steadfastly and scrupulously. Thus, indeed, Our Most Beloved Son, as the Bishops of France wrote so well in the past to your most pious predecessor, it is through the Kingdom on Earth that the Kingdom of Heaven (namely, the Catholic Church) must thrive, so that those
30 within its fold, acting against the faith and discipline of the Church, ought to be rigorously checked by Princes, and the supreme (civil) authority should apply such disciplinary measures as the Church is unable to enforce. Hoping as we do that our effort will not fail, we, in paternal affection, feel it our duty to congratulate you, who have
35 in a very praiseworthy manner so far endeavoured to extirpate similar reproachable errors. . . .

Given at Rome, this tenth day of September 1713, the thirteenth of our Pontificate.

> *Clementis Undecimi Pont. Max. Epistolae et Brevia Selectiora* (Rome, 1724), vol ii, pp 341–2

Questions

a Explain what is meant by 'as you yourself have given us ample scope for hoping' (lines 21–22).
b Identify (i) 'the notorious French book Reflections on the New Testament' (lines 1–2); (ii) its author.
c Account for the revival and spread of Jansenism (i) 'within the Catholic Church' (lines 8–9); (ii) 'in your most flourishing Kingdom' (lines 9–10).
* d What measures were taken to suppress this movement in France *before 1713?*

e What evidence does this extract provide the historian that Clement XI had been utterly disillusioned by the way his earlier Bull *Vineam Domini Sabaoth* had been received in France in 1705?

★ *f* Do you agree that the Jansenist movement was as much hostile to the Jesuits as it was to the excessive growth of royal power? (see document 2)

★ *g* The Bull *Unigenitus Dei Filius* caused 'a long and bitter commotion in the religious life of France'. Comment.

10 A Clear Conscience?

Monday, August 26 [1715], the night was no better. His leg was dressed, and he heard mass. Everyone left the room after the service, but the king detained the Cardinals de Rohan and de Bissy. Mme de Maintenon remained, as she always did, and with her Maréchal de
5 Villeroy, Père Tellier. . . . The king called the two cardinals to him and protested that he died in the faith, and in submission to the Church. Then he added, looking at them, that he was sorry to leave the affairs of the Church in the state they were; that he himself was perfectly ignorant; they knew, and he called them to witness, that he
10 had done all that they wished him to do; it was therefore for them to answer to God for what had been done, whether too much or too little; he protested once more that he charged them with it before God; that his own conscience was clear, as that of an ignorant man who had yielded himself absolutely to them throughout the whole
15 affair. What a fearful thunderbolt! But the two cardinals were not so easily frightened; their calmness was beyond peradventure. They replied with praises and assurances of safety; and again the king repeated that, in his ignorance, he thought he did all for the best in allowing them to guide him, and therefore his responsibility before
20 God would be laid upon them. He added that as to Cardinal de Noailles, God was his witness he did not hate him, and had always been sorry for what he had thought it his duty to do against him.

> *Memoirs of the Duc de Saint-Simon on the Times of Louis XIV and the Regency*, trans. and abridged by K. Prescott Wormeley (Boston, 1899)

Questions

a Identify the persons mentioned in lines 3–5 and explain what you understand by the reference to 'the whole affair' in lines 14–15.

★ *b* In what 'state' were 'the affairs of the Church' in France at the time of Louis' death?

c Is it true to say that Louis 'was perfectly ignorant' (lines 8–9) of the real situation in France, that 'he had done all that' his advisers 'wished him to do' (lines 9–10) and that he 'had yielded himself absolutely to them throughout the whole affair' (lines 14–15)?

d Explain fully the historical background to the last sentence of this extract.

e From your knowledge of the period, how important, do you feel, was the influence of (i) Mme de Maintenon; (ii) Pére Tellier; (iii) Cardinal de Noailles on Louis XIV's decisions?

f Which statements in this extract do you consider in need of checking? Say why and what other sources would you use?

g How does Saint-Simon reveal, in this extract, his own prejudice against Louis XIV?

VI   A Soulless Elegance

Introduction

Unmatched in splendour and grandeur, Versailles, 'the unworthy favourite' (Mme de Sévigné) which 'ruined and bled the nation' (Erlanger), was, in all its artistic manifestation, a living expression of the classical style and taste. 'Only in its immensity and its landscaped gardens did Versailles remain in any sense a Baroque creation' (Maland). To the intellectual and rational qualities of the French Catholic temperament, Baroque, with all its exuberance, fervour and excitement, was a spiritual distraction, evinced in the discomfiture of Bernini's tense sojourn in Paris in the 1660s. The discipline and austerity of the classical tradition, with its scrupulous concern for ceremonial formality, order, restraint and logical clarity, were ideally more congenial to the absolute monarchy of Louis XIV.

France's complete absorption of Classicism was determined by the king's taste and clear vision of beauty. His passion for unity and stability and his obsessive 'horror of disparity' were as much reflected in the artistic sphere as they were in the political, the social and the religious. It was not the function of art 'to excite' but 'to please', not to experiment but to conform through strict observance of the established rules which alone would guarantee harmony and orthodoxy. 'The literature of the period,' says John Lough, was 'essentially *conformiste*; it accepted as wholly natural both the social and political institutions of the time and the dominant religious outlook.'

Under the Sun King the quintessence of art, in its widest sense, 'served to create the image of power and glory for all the world to see and admire' (Hugh Macdonald), 'to provide an appropriate setting' for Louis and his court, and 'to record his actions and the glories of his reign' (A. Blunt). In 1678, at the height of Louis' glory, Racine, *historiographe du Roi*, considered language, indeed every word, every syllable, as a precious instrument of praise 'à la gloire de notre auguste protecteur'.

Rather 'than content,' says Theodore K. Rabb, 'surface qualities,' like a fastidious concern with style, formalised expression and refined social behaviour, became the dominant feature of the Parisian salons and the Academies. The cults of the *honnête gens* and *préciosité* were genuine products of such a social milieu, the exclusive world of *la cour et la ville*. The *honnête hommes* abhorred all forms of excess and cultivated 'exquisite politeness'; the *précieux* established 'exacting standards of delicacy and refinement in matters of taste'.

It was a soulless elegance as distinctly unemotional and academic as it was remote from reality and the rest of France. How much human character and personality, for example, does the canvas of Hyacinthe Rigaud's majestic portrait of Louis XIV (1701) at the Louvre reveal? Compare to this Bernini's white marble bust (1665), later transferred from Rome to Versailles, where the imposing majesty, arrogance and vanity, so characteristic 'of the king who ruled by divine right, accountable only to God', are captured with such accurate precision, such superb 'imagination and intelligence'. It is the man and his proud soul, 'his vibrant personality', that are chiselled to life and not merely the rich texture and the endless flow of his royal robes.

'The art of Louis XIV,' observes Durant, 'was crippled in inventiveness by authority and fell short of that alliance with the people which gave warmth and depth to Gothic art. The harmony of the arts under Louis was impressive, but it sounded too often the same chord, so that at last it became the expression not of an age and a nation, but only of an ego and a court.'

1   The French Language

When Louis XIV died, French had long since become the language of the king, the state, the law, the court, high society, the academies and the world of letters, and might have appeared to be the language of France, but such was not yet the case. Even in Paris, there were
5   some fields left to conquer: it had not fully converted learned circles and was only just beginning to attract the consideration of professors and students and to seem worthy of their station and learning. Furthermore, anybody who moved away from his home region found that the country dwellers and even the inhabitants of the
10   smaller towns either knew no French or understood it without speaking it. While it was meeting next to no resistance in its conquest of Europe, its invasion of France was proceeding painfully slowly, province by province. It still had competitors, and in some places near-rivals, inside the realm. . . .
15   [T]he glamour of the 'great King's' court has dazzled its observers to such a degree that their eyes are rendered almost incapable of discerning the realities, wretched enough, of the rest of the kingdom. The talk at Versailles was so fine that we assume it must have been so everywhere else, and tend to forget that you needed an
20   interpreter in Marseille, or that Racine on his travels was unable to request a chamber-pot.

In any case, Louis XIV was not particularly perturbed at being harangued in Picard patois a few leagues out of Paris, and his successors hardly gave a moment's consideration to such a trifling
25   detail, which in no way diminished the obedience of their subjects or the powers of the monarchy.

> Ferdinand Brunot, *Histoire de la langue française des origines à 1900*, vol vii, *La propagation du français en France jusqu'à la fin de l'Ancien Régime* (Colin, 1926), pp 1–2. Reproduced in Goubert, op cit, pp 277–8

Questions

★   *a*   Suggest plausible reasons why the spread of the French language met 'next to no resistance' (line 11) in Europe but proceeded 'painfully slowly' (line 12) inside France.

 b   What do you understand by 'It still had competitors, and in some places near-rivals, inside the realm' (lines 13–14)?

★   *c*   From Brunot's observations on the French language, what conclusions would you draw on the levels of literacy in French society under Louis XIV?

★   *d*   'When Louis XIV died . . .' (line 1). How does the status of the French language in 1715 reflect upon the absolute monarchy of Louis XIV?

2   An 'Olympiad' near Montpellier, 1676

Men ran at Celleneuve about twelve score yards or something more over ploughed land, very stony, barefoot, and maidens the same, about half so far. There were also races of boys together and girls in other courses. He that won among the men had a hat, among the
5   maidens a ribbon, and less fry smaller matters, all which were given at this annual Olympiad by the Cardinal who is the *seigneur* of the place, and was all tied to the end of a pole which was held up at the end of the race. The whole prize thus exposed was a hat, several ribbons and tagged laces, two or three purses and a few pennies.
10 Jumping also was another exercise, and after all what never fails, dancing to oboe and tabor.

> *Locke's travels in France*, op cit, p 109

Questions

 a   What impression of village life do you get from this passage?

 b   Explain fully and comment on the historical significance of 'and after all what never fails, dancing to oboe and tabor' (lines 10–11).

★   *c*   Discuss briefly the social and psychological importance of activities such as 'this annual Olympiad' (line 6) in seventeenth-century France.

3   Christopher Wren's Impressions of Paris, 1665

I have busied myself in surveying the most esteem'd fabricks of
Paris, and the country round; the Louvre for a while was my daily
object, where no less than a thousand hands are constantly employ'd
in the works; some laying mighty foundations, some in raising the
5   stories, columns, entablements, etc., with vast stones, by great and
useful engines; others in carving, inlaying of marbles, plaistering,
painting, gilding, etc. Which altogether make a school of
architecture, the best probably at this day in Europe. The College of
the Four Nations is usually admir'd, but the artist hath purposely set
10   it ill-favouredly, that he might show his wit in struggling with an
inconvenient situation – An academy of painters, sculptors,
architects, and the other chief artificers of the Louvre, meet every
first and last Saturday of the month. Mons. Colbert, Surintendant,
comes to the works of the Louvre, every Wednesday, and, if
15   business hinders not, Thursday. The workmen are paid every
Sunday duly. Mons. Abbé Charles introduc'd me to the
acquaintance of Bernini, who shew'd me his designs of the Louvre,
and of the King's statue. – Abbé Bruno keeps the curious rarities of
the Duke of Orléan's library, well fill'd with excellent intaglios,
20   medals, books of plants, and fowles in miniature. Abbé Burdelo
keeps an academy at his house of philosophy every Monday
afternoon. – But I must not think to describe Paris, and the
numerous observables there, in the compass of a short letter – The
King's houses I could not miss: Fontainebleau has a stately
25   wilderness and vastness suitable to the desert it stands in. The
antique mass of the Castle of St Germains, and the hanging-gardens
are delightfully surprising . . . for the pleasures below vanish away
in the breath that is spent in ascending. The Palace, or if you please
the Cabinet of Versailles call'd me twice to view it: the mixtures of
30   brick, stone, blue tile and gold make it look like a rich livery: not an
inch within but is crowded with little curiosities of ornaments: the
women, as they make here the language and fashions, and meddle
with politicks and philosophy, so they sway also in architecture;
works of filgrand, and little knacks are in great vogue; but building
35   certainly ought to have the attribute of eternal, and therefore the
only thing uncapable of new fashions. The masculine furniture of
Palais Mazarine pleas'd me much better, where there is a great and
noble collection of antique statues and bustos (many of prophyry)
good basso-rilievos; excellent pictures of the great masters, fine
40   Arras, true mosaicks, besides pierre de rapport in compartiments,
and pavements; vases of porcelain painted by Raphael, and infinite
other rarities; the best of which now furnish the glorious appartment
of the Queen Mother in the Louvre . . . Bernini's design of the
Louvre I would have given my skin for, but the old reserv'd Italian
45   gave me but a few minutes view; it was five little designs in paper,

for which he hath received as many thousand pistoles; I had only time to copy it in my fancy and memory; I shall be able by discourse, and a crayon, to give you a tolerable account of it.

Stephen Wren, *Parentalia, or Memoirs of the Family of the Wrens* (London, 1750), pp 261–3, in Ranum (eds), op cit, pp 197–9

Questions

a Identify (i) Bernini (lines 17 and 43); (ii) Raphael (line 41). Identify the 'College' (line 8) and the 'Four Nations' after which it was named. Why was it so called?

b Explain the historical context of (i) 'an inconvenient situation' (lines 10–11); (ii) Wren's reference to 'the women' in lines 31–4.

c What was Bernini doing in Paris in 1665?

★ d Why were Bernini's 'designs of the Louvre' (line 17), which Wren 'would have given [his] skin for' (line 44), eventually turned down by Colbert?

e Compare and contrast Wren's impressions of Paris in 1665 with Dr Martin Lister's in 1698 (Section II, doc. 10).

4 L'art de plaire

(a) *La Fontaine on his Fables, 1668*

I reflected that unless I could renovate [the fables] with touches which would enhance their flavour, I should be doing nothing at all. That is what is wanted nowadays – novelty and gaiety; and by gaiety I do not mean that which causes laughter, but a certain charm, an
5 attractive turn which can be given to any kind of subject, even the most serious. . . .

Though I have already exceeded the customary length of prefaces, I have not yet explained the structure of my work. An apologue is composed of two parts, of which one may be called its body, and the
10 other its soul. The body is the Fable, and the soul the Moral. Aristotle laid down that fables should never deal either with human beings or plants, but only with animals. There is more propriety than compulsion in this rule, for neither Aesop nor Phaedrus nor any other fabulist has observed it; whereas none has hitherto dispensed
15 with the moral. I have sometimes done so myself, but only where I could not bring it in gracefully, and the reader could easily supply it. In France nothing matters but to please – that is the great, and in a manner of speaking the only rule. I have therefore not thought it a crime to disregard the ancient conventions when I could not employ
20 them to advantage.

Extract from Jean de La Fontaine, *Preface to the Fables. La Fontaine's Fables*, op cit, pp xi, xiii

(b) Racine on Pierre Corneille, 1685

You know in what a condition the stage was when [Pierre Corneille] began to write. . . . All the rules of art, and even those of decency and decorum, broken everywhere . . . Corneille, after having for some time sought the right path and struggled against the bad taste of his day, inspired by extraordinary genius and helped by the study of the ancients, at last brought reason upon the stage.

> Jean Racine, 'Discours prononcé a l'Académie Française a la reception de M. de Corneille', in *Oeuvres de J. Racine*, ed. Paul Mesnard, vol iv (Paris, 1886), p 336. Reproduced in translation in T. K. Rabb, *The Struggle for Stability in Early Modern Europe* (New York, Oxford University Press, 1975), pp 101–2

25

Questions

a From your knowledge of the social history of this period, what, do you think, is meant by 'That is what is wanted nowadays – novelty and gaiety' (line 3)?

★ b What purpose did 'prefaces' (line 7) to literary works serve in seventeenth-century France? How important are they as historical sources?

c Identify (i) Aristotle (line 11); (ii) Aesop (line 13); (iii) Phaedrus (line 13); (iv) 'the ancient conventions' (line 19).

d Explain and comment briefly on (i) 'There is more propriety than compulsion in this rule' (lines 12–13); (ii) 'In France nothing matters but to please' (line 17).

e What does extract *a* tell us about La Fontaine's attitude towards the 'ancients'? How far, do you think, do his remarks conform to the tastes of the *honnête homme*?

f From your knowledge of this period, explain fully and comment on the historical significance and importance of the first three lines of extract *b*.

★ g What light does Racine's extract shed on the progression that had taken place in Corneille's artistic lifetime?

★ h In view of the hostile criticism which Corneille's masterpiece, *El Cid*, had provoked when it was first performed at the Théâtre du Marais in 1637, how reliable and important as a contemporary source to the cultural historian is Racine's 'eulogy'?

★ i 'Corneille had formed himself alone; but Louis XIV, Colbert, Sophocles and Euripides all contributed to form Racine' (Voltaire). In the light of this quotation, discuss the two extracts in an attempt to distinguish clearly between 'evolution' and 'imposition' of forms of taste in French society during the *grand siècle*.

5 Theatrical Performances

(a) 11 [May 1651]. I went to the *Palas Cardinal* where the Master of Ceremonies plac'd me to see the royal *Masque*: The first sceane represented a Charriot of Singers, composed of the rarest voices to be procur'd, representing *Cornaro* & Temperance: This was overthrowne by *Bacchus* & his Revellers, the rest consisted of severall enteries, & pageants of Excesse, by all the Elements: A Masque representing fire was admirable: Then came a *Venus* out the Clouds etc. The Conclusion was an heaven whither all ascended. But the glory of the Masque was the greate persons performing it, namely the *French* King. . . . The *King* performing to the admiration of all: The Musique was 24 Violins, vested al' antique; but the habites of the Masquers were stupendiously rich & glorious.

> *The Diary of John Evelyn*, op cit, pp 300–1

(b) In the afternoon I heard a Comedy at Palais-Royal. They were Monseir's Comedians; they had a farce after it. I gave Quinze Solz to stand upon the grounde. The name of it was *Coeur de Mari*. They were not to be compared with the Londoners.

> Edward Browne, 1664. *A Journal of a Visit to Paris in the year 1664*, ed. G. Keynes (London, 1923), p 16

(c) Palais Cardinal is a fair palace with handsome walks. Here Madame Henrietta, the duchess of Orleans, lives. At one side of this house is a public stage where the Italian and French comedians act by turns. I saw here *Il maritaggion d'una Statua*, a merry play where the famous buffoon, Scaramuccio, acted. Three antick dances pleased the spectators. The *Quatre Scaramuccie* was another pleasant Italian comedy. We stood in the parterre, or pit, and paid 30 sols a piece for seeing the first, and but 15 sols for the last.
We saw a French comedy entitled *L'estourdye* which was better acted than we expected. We paid for seeing this, and standing in the pit, 15 sols a man.

> Philip Skippon, 1666. *An Account of a Journey through part of the Low Countries, Germany, Italy and France* in *A Collection of Voyages and Travels*, vol vi (London, 1732), p 731

(d) I cannot tell you the extreme beauty [of Racine's *Esther* at St Cyr]: it is a performance not easy to represent, and is inimitable: it is the union of music, poetry, singing, and character, so perfect and complete, that there is nothing we wish to alter. The young ladies who represent kings and great personages, seem to be made on purpose. It commands attention, and the only unpleasant circumstance attending it is, that so fine a production should at last end. Everything in it is simple and innocent, sublime and affecting: the sacred history is so faithfully adhered to, as to create respect; all

the airs corresponding with the words, which are taken from the
Psalms or *Ecclesiastes*, and interwoven with the subject, are singularly
beautiful; the taste and attention of the audience are the criterions of
the merit of the piece. . . . The King approached our seat, and
having turned round, addressed himself to me: 'I am told, Madame,'
said he, 'that the piece has given you satisfaction.' I replied, with
perfect self-possession, 'Sire, I am delighted; what I feel is beyond
the power of words to describe.' The King continued, 'Racine has
great talents.' I replied, 'Sire, he has indeed; and so have these young
people: they enter into the subject, as if it had been their sole
employment.' 'Ah! that is very true,' he rejoined. And he then
retired, leaving me the object of universal envy.

  Madame de Sévigné, 21 February 1689. *Letters*, op cit, vol vi,
   pp 223–4

Questions

a What impression do you get from these extracts of (i) the king;
  (ii) French society; (iii) the French theatre?

★ *b* Suggest reasons why French actors, in Browne's opinion, 'were
  not to be compared with the Londoners' (line 16), and why
  Skippon should have 'expected' them not to play as well as they
  in fact did.

c Explain and comment on the historical background to these
  references: (i) 'the greate persons performing it' (line 9); (ii)
  'Monseir's Comedians' (line 14); (iii) 'the Italian and French
  comedians act by turns' (lines 19–20).

★ *d* Comment briefly on the function of Saint Cyr and the relation to
  it of the 'young ladies' in line 31.

e What literary merits do you find in Madame de Sévigné's *lettre*
  (extract *d*)? Are they typical or atypical of Louis XIV's age 'when
  civilisation was somewhat artificial and conventional' (Ogg)?

f 'By mentioning the circumstance to which she believed she was
  indebted for this little favour of the King, she proves sufficiently
  that she was not so much elated with it as has been pretended'
  (Newton). Discuss briefly lines 40–48 in the light of this
  quotation.

g What impressions of the social composition of the audience did
  you get from a close reading of these four extracts?

6 'The chosen instrument of Louis' musical glory'

(a) French composers would be terrified that disaster would follow
if they ventured on the slightest deviation from the rules. They were
all for soothing and caressing the ear; the ear was their god, and, even
when they had done their utmost to obey the rules, they were still

5   haunted by the fear that, for all their care, they might have done
     something amiss. The Italians are bolder than that. They will make
     abrupt changes of key and time, give the most numerous and
     complicated trills to notes we should think incapable of sustaining
     the slightest shake. They will sustain one single note for such a time
10   that people not used to it get impatient at what they first think an
     outrage, but afterwards cannot sufficiently admire.

> Raguenet, *Parallele des italiens et des français en ce qui regarde la ·*
> *musique et les opéras*, 1702

(b) Between 1673 and his death in 1687 [Jean–Baptiste] Lully wrote
about one opera a year, and these works were to dominate the French
repertory for nearly a century. It was remarkable that this should
15   have so come about, since Lully's music has never had abundant
admirers and could never be compared in genius to contemporaries
such as Purcell or Alessandro Scarlatti, nor to his great successor
Rameau. Since the eighteenth century his operas have remained
quite dead, untouched even by the modern taste for baroque
20   revivals. This perhaps indicates how indissolubly the Lullian
tragédie-lyrique was linked to the tastes and circumstances of its time
and its nation, representing an aspect of the *grand siècle* that cannot
again be brought to life. The monarchy is itself present in the music,
for Quinault, who supplied Lully with a dozen libretti, would
25   submit certain subjects, usually drawn from Ovidian mythology, to
the king, who would select one which he approved. The Prologue in
these works is an undisguised panegyric of the king, often making
reference to notable events of the day and elevating his heroic
· virtues: triumphant in war, generous in peace. The action of the
30   operas circles round themes of glory and love. Monsters are
overcome and enemies are magnanimously defeated. In the Preface
to *Persée* (1682) Lully declared: 'I understand that in describing the
favourable gifts which Persée has received from the Gods and the
astonishing enterprises which he has achieved so gloriously, I am
35   tracing a portrait of the heroic qualities and the wonderful deeds of
Your Majesty.'

Lully based his style on the breadth and firmness that
magniloquence demands, best seen in the opening sections of his
overtures. Although he perhaps drew it from an Italian model,
40   Lully's 'French overture' became accepted all over Europe with its
bracing dotted rhythms followed by fugal or flowing second
sections. . . . Lully also devised a distinct style of recitative based on
theatrical declamation, entirely different from that of Italian opera.
He took pains to reproduce the flow and accent of tragic
45   declamation. 'If you wish to sing my music correctly,' he said, 'go
and hear la Champmesté.' . . . Lully's recitative constantly
alternates in time signature and bar length in order to catch the stress
of the words, using a strictly syllabic style, and he was adept at

alternating recitative and air or *ariette* in a way which Italians, with
0 their stricter segregation of recitative and aria, would never accept.
French opera did not allow singers and singing to dominate the stage
as they did in Italy, and the extensive dramatic personae of the
Lullian *tragédie-lyrique*, often incorporating numerous deities or
minor personages, reflects much more care for theatrical than vocal
5 splendour. None the less characteristic French voices were
cultivated. Where the Italians had their splendid *castrati*, the usual
heroic voice in France was the *haute-contre*, singing in the highest
tenor range. The *haute-contre* survived into the nineteenth century as
the high lyric tenor.

H. Macdonald, 'French Music since 1500', in *France: A
Companion to French Studies*, ed. D. G. Charlton, 2nd edn
(London, Methuen, 1979), pp 546–7

Questions

a   Explain fully the historical significance of Raguenet's reference
to 'the rules' in line 2.

b   Identify (i) Purcell (line 17); (ii) Alessandro Scarlatti (line 17); (iii)
Rameau (line 18); (iv) Quinault (line 24); (v) Champmesté (line
46).

c   With reference to both extracts, explain fully, in your own
words, what distinguished French from Italian music during the
grand siècle.

d   What do you understand by (i) *tragédie-lyrique* (lines 21 and 53);
(ii) *castrati* (line 56); (iii) *haute-contre* (lines 57 and 58)?

e   'The monarchy is itself present in the music' (line 23). How did
Lully succeed in expressing Louis XIV's 'musical glory'?

★ f   'The Parisian public greatly preferred Lully's Italianate music,
with its concessions to French sensibility, to Cavalli's original
and essentially Italian work, whose boldness and vehemence of
expression seemed to be an affront to good taste and to reason'.
Discuss Macdonald's assessment of Lully's music in the light of
this quotation.

g   What explanation does Macdonald suggest for the fact that
Lully's operas 'have remained quite dead' since the eighteenth
century, 'untouched even by the modern taste for baroque
revivals' (lines 18–20)?

7   La Rochefoucauld

(a) Maximes

(i) The evil we do brings less persecution and hatred upon us than
our good qualities.
(ii) We have not the strength to follow our reason all the way.

(iii) Although men pride themselves on their noble deeds, these are
5   seldom the outcome of a grand design but simply effects of chance.
(iv) Simple grace is to the body what common sense is to the mind.
(v) What makes us so unstable in our friendships is that it is difficult
to get to know qualities of soul but easy to see those of the mind.
(vi) To disillusion a man convinced of his own worth is to do him as
10   bad a turn as they did to that Athenian madman who thought all the
vessels entering the harbour were his.
(vii) Courtesy of the mind consists in thinking kind and delicate
thoughts.
(viii) One of the reasons why so few people are to be found who
15   seem sensible and pleasant in conversation is that almost everybody
is thinking about what he wants to say himself rather than about
answering clearly what is being said to him. The more clever and
polite think it enough simply to put on an attentive expression, while
all the time you can see in their eyes and train of thought that they are
20   far removed from what you are saying and anxious to get back to
what they want to say. They ought, on the contrary, to reflect that
such keenness to please oneself is a bad way of pleasing or persuading
others, and that to listen well and answer to the point is one of the
most perfect qualities one can have in conversation.
25   (ix) The glory of great men must always be measured against the
means they have used to acquire it.
(x) Only the great are entitled to great faults.
(xi) We should often blush at our noblest deeds if the world were to
see all their underlying motives.
30   (xii) Kings turn men into coins to which they assign what value they
like, and which others are obliged to accept at the official rate, and
not at their real worth.

> La Rochefoucauld, *Maxims*, trans. Leonard Tancock
> (Penguin, reprint 1984), nos 29, 42, 57, 67, 80, 92, 99, 139,
> 157, 190, 409, 603. The first edition of the *Maximes* appeared
> in Paris in 1665.

(b) Voltaire on the 'Maximes'

One of the works which most contributed to form the taste of the
nation and gave it a spirit of nicety and precision was the little
35   collection of *Maxims* by François, Duke de La Rochefoucauld.
Although there is but one little truth expressed in this book, namely,
that 'self-love is the mainspring of every action,' yet the thought is
presented under so many various aspects, that it is nearly always
striking. It is not so much a book as materials to embellish a book.
40   The little collection was read with eagerness; and it accustomed
people to think and to express their thoughts in a vivid, concise and
elegant manner. It was a merit which no other writer had had before
in Europe, since the revival of letters.

> Voltaire, op cit, p 358

a Who was La Rochefoucauld?

b Which of these maxims, do you feel, apply to Louis XIV, and which to the artificial life of the salons? Explain fully why.

★ *c* What advantages would reflections such as La Rochefoucauld's *Maximes*, 'with often no connected thread', enjoy over 'logically constructed works'?

★ *d* What, do you think, was the author's ultimate intention in composing these *Maximes*?

e In the light of extract *b*, what main stylistic features characterised this form of writing? Illustrate your answer from the maxims in extract *a*.

f From a close reading of the twelve maxims in extract *a*, arrive at a definition of the *honnête homme* concept.

8   Versailles: the unworthy favourite

Who could count [Louis XIV's] buildings? At the same time, who would not deplore the pride, the capriciousness and the bad taste so evident in them? He abandoned Saint-Germain and built nothing ornamental or convenient in Paris except Port Royal, and this out of
5   sheer necessity. Paris is inferior to many cities all over Europe. . . .
He abandoned [Saint-Germain, a unique site which commands a superb view] for Versailles, the dullest and most unworthy of places, without views, woods, water or soil as everywhere around is shifting sand or swamp. Nor is there as a result any fresh air. He
10   enjoyed subduing nature by art and treasures. Everything he built [at Versailles] betrays no general design: the beautiful and the ugly, the vast and the mean were all stuck together. His and the Queen's apartments are extremely inconvenient, overlooking dull, close and foul-smelling areas. The gardens, surprisingly magnificent, are also
15   regretfully in bad taste. Only by passing through a vast torrid zone can one enjoy the cool freshness of the shade. . . . The violence done everywhere to nature is both repelling and disgusting. The abundance of water [was artificially] channelled from all directions . . . causing unhealthy humidity and an even worse odour. . . .
20   But the water supply was constantly defective in spite of the sealike reservoirs which incurred so many millions to construct upon the shifting sand and mud. Who would have believed it? Madame de Maintenon was then reigning . . . M. de Louvois was on good terms with her. It was a time of peace. He conceived the idea of
25   diverting the River Eure between Chartres and Maintenon and redirecting it entirely to Versailles. Who can say what gold and men this obstinate attempt cost over the years, since it was strictly forbidden, under severe penalties, in the [military] camp which had been established there . . . to speak of the sick – and of the dead in

30 particular – which the hard labour had caused? How many others took long years to recover from the contagion! How many were never to regain their health at all! [Work] was interrupted by the war in 1688 . . . and all that remains is a shapeless monument which will render this cruel folly eternal.

Mémoires de Saint-Simon, ed. A. Cheruel (Paris, 1857), vol xii

Questions

a   Explain the historical significance of (i) 'out of sheer necessity' (lines 4–5); (ii) 'The violence done everywhere to nature' (lines 16–17); (iii) 'water was artificially channelled from all directions' (line 18); (iv) 'It was a time of peace' (line 24).

★ b   From your knowledge of the reign, comment briefly on Saint-Simon's remark that Louis XIV 'built nothing ornamental or convenient in Paris' (lines 3–4).

c   To what extent and for what reasons is it correct to say that in Louis XIV's reign Paris was 'inferior to many cities all over Europe' (line 5)?

d   How does Saint-Simon support his view that Versailles was 'the dullest and most unworthy of places' (line 7)?

e   Why does Saint-Simon call Versailles a 'cruel folly' (line 34)?

★ f   Saint-Simon 'was a man of unlimited prejudice' (Judge). From your historical knowledge, do you consider Saint-Simon's view of Versailles prejudiced? Explain fully why.

★ g   Discuss briefly the reliability and importance of Saint-Simon, 'the best memorialist of the reign', as historical evidence.

9   Painting

The doctrine of the [Académie de Peinture et de Sculpture], based as it was on the models of antiquity, Raphael and Poussin, further laid down that drawing was the true basis of painting, because it appealed to the mind, and that colour, which only appealed to the eye, was of
5   altogether minor importance. This doctrine soon aroused opposition and led to a series of violent discussions between the supporters of drawing, called the *Poussinistes*, and the partisans of colour, called the *Rubénistes*, because they set up Rubens as the equal of the great French painter on account of his mastery of colour. The
10   drawing-colour quarrel was in many ways a parallel to the Quarrel of the Ancients and the Moderns, in that it involved a challenge to the supremacy of ancient sculpture and of the masters who based their art on the study of it. It was also connected with a new naturalism in painting, because one of the arguments in favour of
15   colour was that it produced a more complete imitation of natural objects than was possible by drawing alone. In the end the supporters of colour, led by the critic Roger de Piles, won the day,

and the tradition of classical idealism inaugurated by Poussin and
carried on by Lebrun and the Academy gave way to a quite different
20   conception of painting.

Anthony Blunt, 'French Painting, Sculpture and
Architecture since 1500', in Charlton, op cit, p 498

Questions

a   Identify (i) the 'Académie de Peinture et de Sculpture' (line 1); (ii)
     Poussin (line 2); (iii) Rubens (line 8); (iv) Lebrun (line 19).
★   b   Why are Raphael and Poussin called 'the models of antiquity' in
     line 2?
c   What was the 'series of violent discussions' (line 6) all about?
d   Explain fully and comment on the historical significance of 'the
     Quarrel of the Ancients and the Moderns' (lines 10–11). In what
     ways was the *Poussinistes-Rubénistes* controversy 'parallel' to this
     quarrel?

VII Things Fall Apart

Introduction

The Peace of Nijmegen and the succeeding years of the *réunions* and annexations marked the apogee of Louis XIV's glory and prosperity. The League of Augsburg marked a decisive turning point in his fortunes (Acton). The Ottoman rout outside Vienna and the recapture of Hungary not only strengthened Leopold I's confidence and morale; it shattered Louis' hopes of installing a Bourbon on the Habsburg 'throne of Charlemagne'. If the major motive behind the Revocation of the Edict of Nantes had been Louis' desire to regain 'the initiative in Catholic Europe', it failed. Indeed, both Catholic and Protestant Europe demonstrated in Augsburgian concert its hostility to the megalomaniac king. His devastation of the Palatinate – 'most barbarously ruined' (Evelyn); 'the pivotal mistake of [Louis'] military career' (Durant); 'the most fateful of all the "atrocities" committed during the reign of Louis XIV' (Wolf) – was, and still is, a matter of controversy. 'I must represent to His Majesty,' a French general wrote to Louvois, 'the bad effect which such a desolation may make upon the world in respect to his glory and reputation.' Would it not have been wiser, perhaps, if Louis' troops 'marched against Maastricht' instead of Philippsburg? This would have had the triple advantage of forestalling William of Orange, his 'leading opponent', aiding his Roman Catholic ally, James II, and not alienating Saxony, Hanover and Brunswick, his German allies.

Equally controversial are the causes of the Peace of Ryswick, when France for the first time lost ground. Was Louis XIV's grand display of moderation at Ryswick inspired by his malicious intent to procure 'the throne of Spain for [his] grandson'? Voltaire discards this 'supposition' downright as 'false'. Peace, he remarks, 'was made out of weariness of war' and 'the exhausted state of his finances'. Briggs similarly believes that the 'financial strength of London and Amsterdam enabled the allies to outlast French resources, finally exhausted by the terrible harvest year of 1693–4'. Treasure views the question differently: 'neither military stalemate nor economic stress alone account for Louis' apparent modesty'. The 'trente-deux villes / Et Luxembourg' meant nothing by comparison with 'that great [Spanish] inheritance'. And again Voltaire: 'The obvious importance of obtaining a part or the whole of Spain at an early date did not influence the Peace of Ryswick in the slightest.' Quite recently Maland observes: 'Louis was prepared to accept the losses of 1697 in order to realise his dream of peaceably acquiring the Spanish Empire, which at long last, seemed to be within his grasp.'

The remaining years of Louis' reign were occupied as much by 'the lengthening shadow of the Spanish succession' (Acton) as by sustained opposition, more bitter and more outspoken than hitherto experienced, both from the *Camisards*, the fanatical Huguenot peasants of the Cevennes district, who stubbornly resisted submission to the Catholic faith, and, more surprisingly, from among the king's own trusted aristocratic circles. 'You are praised to the skies,' wrote Fénelon in a letter to the *grand monarque*, 'for having impoverished France, and you have built your throne on the ruin of all classes in the state.' Vauban's *Projet d'une dîme royale* was another hostile attack on a system which, based on the principle of privilege, was seen as the source of the economic misery of the population.

Charles II, the childless king of Spain, died on 1 November 1700. Louis XIV, 'the French protagonist of partition', accepted the 'undivided inheritance' in Charles II's last Will, which declared Philip of Anjou, second son of the Dauphin of France, as the sole heir of the Spanish monarchy in its integrity. Can Louis be really blamed for going back on a treaty which he had only just concluded with England and Holland, and which would have transferred 'the whole Spanish succession to his Austrian rival'? It is debatable if this act alone, the prospect of a Bourbon in Madrid, made war inevitable. 'A general European conflict might still have been avoided if Louis XIV had shown himself less high-handed at the moment of triumph' (Elliott). It was 'the new spirit of arrogant intemperance which the will created in his mind' (Fisher), his 'overbearing arrogance which had antagonised every vested interest in Europe' which, on 7 September 1701, revived the formidable Grand Alliance and precipitated a general European war against France which was to last until 1713. It was the series of '[decisive] hammer blows' which the hitherto invincible French forces suffered during the long, protracted course of the war of the Spanish succession – Blenheim, Ramillies, Turin, Oudenarde, Lille, Malplaquet – that ultimately sealed the fate of Louis *le grand*.

Madame de Maintenon had on one occasion allegedly confessed to her husband that 'Princes never want to look at misfortune; they are accustomed to having these things hidden from them'. Although France had been spared 'the losses and indignities that had been threatened' (Wolf) three or four years before Utrecht, 'the scale and importance of the defeat could not be hidden. Louis XIV had the misfortune to live long enough to see the consequences of his own errors, with the destruction of French claims to preponderance in Europe' (Briggs).

1   A Scorching Policy

(a) Louvois to M. du Montal, Versailles, 18 February 1684

Sir,

The King having been informed that the Spaniards put to the torch
two barns full of fodder and grain situated at the extremities of the
villages of Avenelle and Sepmenier, in the administrative district of
5 Avesnes, His Majesty commanded me to inform you that he wishes
you to burn twenty villages as close as possible to Charleroi, and that
you distribute handbills saying that it is in retaliation for the burning
of these two barns; the King's will is that Gauchelys, Guernets, and
Fleuru be among their number, and that you take the necessary steps
10 in carrying this out so that not a single house in these twenty villages
remains standing; that in the future at the first notification you
receive of a similar thing, you will act in like manner without
awaiting further orders from His Majesty; that the above should be
carried out by a large detachment, which His Majesty wishes you to
15 command yourself, and which is substantial enough so that there
need be no fear of the joining of the garrisons of Namur and of
Charleroi.

(b) Louvois to M. de Montbron, Versailles, 21 February 1684

Sir,

There are many villages which have not yet paid the demands which
20 have been made upon them last year and this year; the King's will is
that you punish with the utmost severity those who do not finally
pay at once; His Majesty expects that after having so precisely
directed you (to do so) he will be obeyed to the letter, since his
service requires that the Spanish territories be entirely ravaged, or
25 that everything that he has asked of them be paid before the end of
the coming month.

> Letters of Louvois, ed. J. Hardre (Chapel Hill, University of
> North Carolina, 1949), in Ranum (eds), op cit, pp 276–7

Questions

   a '[T]he most feared, hated, and respected official in the French
      government' (Ranum). In what way is this image of Louvois
      borne out by the content and tone of these two letters?

★ *b* What was the ultimate purpose of Louis XIV's (or Louvois')
      'scorching policy'?

★ *c* Judged from its results, how effective did such a policy prove to
      be eventually?

   d What impression do you get from these letters of the state and
      reputation of France's military forces in the early 1680s?

2 Louis XIV's Designs Discovered

Henry the Eighth, king of England, did in his time cause a medal to be stamped, with a hand stretched out of a cloud holding a balance in equipoise, whereof both the scales represented Spain and France, with this motto, *Cui adhaereo praeest*, i.e., My alliance weighs it
5 down. It seems that prince well knew his own might, whereas now England may be compared to an ox, who, being insensible of his own strength, quietly submits himself to the yoke. Evident it is that England has many advantages beyond other kingdoms, but especially this, that being an island it can easily secure itself against
10 any foreign force. They that intend an invasion against it must be obliged to cross the seas, and struggle with the winds and waves and all the hazards and dangers of that unstable element, besides a very potent fleet which alone is sufficient to deter their hardiest enemy from any such design. Now this being so, it is manifest that the king
15 of England (having peace and a strict alliance with Holland) can overbalance the party he designs against.

This is a truth France is so fully convinced of that, notwithstanding the great antipathy there is between both nations, he has hitherto spared nothing, and is still turning every stone, to
20 take off England from its true interest and to engage it on his side, or at least to oblige it to stand neuter, and to be an idle, unconcerned spectator of the horrid tragedy the French king acts upon the theatre of Europe, because he well knows that England is better able to prevent it, and spoil his sport, than any other state or kingdom
25 whatsoever, and rescue Europe from the universal slavery he prepares for it. Would the king of England only be pleased to open his eyes, fast closed with the enchanted slumbers of the French Delilah, to take a view of his own strength and true interest, he should soon find himself making another figure amongst the princes
30 of Europe than of late years he hath done, and with ease mount that high degree of power and glory of being the professed umpire of the universe, the sovereign mediator and decider of controversies and the giver of peace to all Europe, which France in vain bravado pretends to, when indeed he is the sole troubler of it.

35 To arrive at this transcendent pitch of grandeur and authority two things only (which the king of England may do when he pleases) are requisite. The first is that his Majesty do comport himself so as to engage the love of his people, and keep a right understanding between him and his Parliament; and the second that he enter into a
40 strict alliance with Holland, living in sincere amity, perfect union and good correspondence with them, in order to their common defence and security. The former of these is very easy, and the king will do it as soon as he shall resolve to desire nothing of his Parliament but what is agreeable with the laws of the realm . . .; and
45 the latter will be found to be of absolute necessity as soon as the king

of England shall please to stop his ears to the false suggestions of France. . . .

That there can be nothing so evidently destructive of the French designs as this union between England and Holland is very apparent.
50 England can, when it pleases, overturn the projects of France against the Spanish Netherlands. Neither could that king ever have taken Luxemburg if the late king of England had had the least inclination to oppose him in that attempt; but the French king so well knew how to take him by the blind side that he did not perceive the mischief till the
55 city was taken. It was a capital error for England to part with Dunkirk, a place that opened a passage for them to France and the Low Countries; but it would make the matter much worse if all those countries should be fain to submit to the tyranny of Louis the Great, and he by this means should join Newport and Ostend in
60 Dunkirk, for then would Flushing follow by consequence, and that king be put into a condition to dispute the sovereignty of the sea with his British Majesty, and destroy the navigation and commerce of this flourishing kingdom. Having got thus far he would proceed to an entire conquest of the United Provinces, which point being once
65 gained by him, England would have but little reason to flatter itself with the hopes of a better lot. . . .

> 'The Designs of France against England and Holland Descovered', an anonymous pamphlet, dated 1686, denouncing the French, in *Harleian Miscellany*, ed. R. Dutton (London, 1808–11), vol ix, pp 164–7

Questions

a Explain the historical significance of 'now England may be compared . . . the yoke' (lines 5–7), and comment briefly on its validity.

★ b Account for the 'great antipathy' (line 18) between France and England in 1686. How serious was Louis XIV's threat to Europe then?

★ c '[I]s still turning every stone' (line 19). What measures was Louis XIV taking in the 1680s to keep England away 'from its true interest or to engage it on his side, or at least to oblige it to stand neuter' (lines 20–21)?

d Explain and comment on the historical aptness of the 'Delilah' image in lines 26–8.

★ e '[T]wo things only . . . are requisite' (lines 35–7). How far do lines 42–4 convey an accurate picture of conditions in England? In what ways, do you think, would the realisation of the first 'requisite' strengthen England's position vis-à-vis the French challenge?

★ f What were France's 'projects . . . against the Spanish Netherlands' (lines 50–1) in 1686?

g Explain the historical background to the author's reference to (i) Luxemburg (line 52); (ii) Dunkirk (line 56).

3 The French Devastation of the Palatinate

(a) An eye-witness report, Kirrweiler, 15 June 1689

On 1 June [1689] the fire caught the houses in the market place and progressed towards the church of St James and the Horse Market. About ten o'clock a fearful thunderstorm and wind arose which spread the fire with terrible rapidity, so that in an instant it was
5 raging in the Herdgasse, and reached the White Tower. Between eleven and twelve it enveloped the Wolzhausen and the whole neighbourhood, for the wind scattered a shower of sparks everywhere, and so it came about that the bell tower of the cathedral was set on fire. This was extinguished no less than three times, but
10 the cloisters were ignited by incendiaries and the near-by buildings caught. . . .
  On the fifth [of June], I learned that an order had arrived to mine and blow up the towers of the cathedral as well as the buildings attached. I went immediately to Marshal Duras at Odenheim to get
15 the order countermanded, and succeeded finally. I wished then to see with my own eyes the ruin of the noble building, and found it, alas, in a worse state than had been reported to me. The vaulting of the nave had wholly collapsed, the building full of rubbish; and chairs, altars, and everything that had been stored there was reduced to
20 ashes. The sacristy and other portions that had escaped the fire had been plundered.
  Reproduced in Ranum (eds), op cit, pp 279–80

(b) Voltaire's account

In February 1689, an order was issued to the army by Louis, signed by Louvois, to reduce the country to ashes. It was in the heart of winter; the French generals could not but obey, and accordingly
25 announced to the citizens of all those flourishing and well-ordered towns, to the inhabitants of the villages, and to the masters of more than fifty castles, that they would have to leave their homes, which were to be destroyed by fire and sword. Men, women, old people and children departed in haste. Some went wandering about the
30 countryside; others sought refuge in neighbouring countries, while the soldiery, who always carry out to the letter orders of exceptional severity and fail to observe more merciful ones, burnt and sacked their country. They began with Mannheim and Heidelberg, the seats of the Electors; their palaces as well as the houses of common citizens
35 were destroyed; their tombs were opened by the rapacious soldiery, who thought to find treasures there; and their ashes were scattered.

For the second time this beautiful country was ravaged by Louis
XIV, but the flames of the two towns and twenty villages which
Turenne had burnt in the Palatinate were but sparks compared with
40 this conflagration. Europe was horror-struck. The officers who
executed the orders were ashamed to be the instruments of such
severity. They placed the responsibility on the Marquis de Louvois,
who had become less humane through that hardening of sensibilities
which a lengthy ministry produces. He had indeed advised this
45 course, but Louis had been master enough not to agree to it. Had the
king been a witness of the sight he would himself have extinguished
the flames. Within the precincts of his palace at Versailles and in the
midst of pleasures, he signed the destruction of an entire country;
and he saw in this order nothing but his own power and the
50 unfortunate prerogative of war; but as an eye-witness he could have
seen nothing but its horror. Nations which until then had only
blamed his ambition while they admired it, now cried out against his
severity and even blamed his policy; for should his enemies invade
his country as he had invaded his enemies', they would likewise burn
55 his cities to the ground.

The danger was a real one; by posting his frontiers with a hundred
thousand men Louis had prompted Germany to similar efforts.

    Voltaire, op cit, p 149

Questions

a Explain the historical meaning of 'For the second time . . .
   conflagration' (lines 37–40).
b Explain and comment on the historical significance of 'Nations
   which until then . . . his policy' (lines 51–3).
c What light do these two extracts shed on (i) Louis XIV; (ii)
   Louvois; (iii) the relationship between the king and his secretary
   of state for war?
★ d What was the purpose behind Louvois' destruction of the Rhine
   Palatinate? What objective did he hope to achieve? Discuss briefly
   the immediate and long-term results of this 'devastation'.
e How accurate and fair do you consider Voltaire's comment on
   the events described in extract a?
★ f '[O]thers sought refuge in neighbouring countries' (line 30).
   What contemporary and later importance would you attribute to
   'tales of distress' such as the eye-witness's report in extract a?

4 'Whoever . . . trusts . . . France is . . . stupid'

But since [the Peace of the Pyrenees] was broken and trampled
underfoot at the first opportunity, it must be recognised that
whoever henceforth trusts the word of France is very stupid, and
deserves to be deceived. That is why the Dutch, the Spanish, the

5   Emperor and the other allies who negotiated at Nimwegen will sooner or later be punished for their credulity.

    If they believed that the French would not encroach upon the Empire and the Low Countries more in the midst of peace than in war, they must have been very blind, or else they preferred fighting
10   together to perishing singly. If we recall the beginning of the recent war, was there anything more outrageous than the manner in which the Duke of Lorraine was despoiled of his state? His sole crime was that he did not wish to be at the mercy of some French governor or intendant, and that he attempted to preserve his security by
15   defensive alliances, the most innocent in the world. The war against the Dutch was so far removed from any appearance of reason (I speak as an enemy of France) that no one was ever able to find a pretext. Yet all the violence which France has perpetrated since then in Germany, in the Low Countries and elsewhere has been excused
20   simply as the necessary sequel to that war. It was for this reason that the French armies traversed Germany (in order to draw away any help that might arrive for the Dutch or serve as a diversion for the French), that they have taken Trier, surprised and dismantled ten cities in Alsace in a manner which hardly resembled good faith, and
25   carried out all sorts of hostilities in the Palatinate of the Rhine, all because of the merest suspicions sanctioned only by the rationale of war, the most unjust war that was ever undertaken. They had the insolence to insist that the Emperor first withdraw his troops from imperial territory, and that the king [Louis] would do the same only
30   when the Emperor had given his word . . . that he would never move outside his hereditary estates; that is to say, the King of France has greater authority in the Empire than did the Emperor himself. Everyone should remain quiet and trust the word of the French ministers who were preaching far and wide that their king sought
35   nothing through war but to rebuke some unknown insolence of the Dutch, as though the desire might not come to him to humiliate others in their turn. . . . We have seen that his aims went further than mere bravado, that he made sure of keeping outposts on the lower Rhine by installing strong garrisons in them, that the crime of
40   the Dutch was their having prevented the occupation of the entire Low Countries, and that the ambition of the king was quite egocentric and contemplated as much profit as glory.

> Gottfried Wilhelm Leibnitz, *Mars Christianissimus, Autore Germano Gallo-Graeco, ou Apologie des Armes du Roy tres-chrestien contre les chrestiens* (Cologne, 1684), reproduced in translation in W. F. Church, *The Greatness of Louis XIV: Myth or Reality?* (Problems in European Civilization) (Boston, D. C. Heath, 1959), p 10

a   Who was Gottfried Wilhelm Leibnitz?

★   b   What was the Peace of the Pyrenees and why does the author say
that it was 'broken and trampled underfoot at the first
opportunity' (lines 1–2)?

c   What do you understand by the first sentence of the second
paragraph?

d   Explain and comment briefly on the historical context of (i) the
author's reference to the Duke of Lorraine in lines 10–15; (ii) 'the
French armies traversed Germany' (line 21); (iii) 'that they have
taken Trier' (line 23); (iv) 'surprised and dismantled ten cities in
Alsace' (lines 23–4); (v) 'They had the insolence . . . hereditary
estates' (lines 27–31).

e   Explain briefly, in your own words, the impression Leibnitz
entertains of Louis XIV and his foreign policy in this extract.

f   'I speak as an enemy of France' (lines 16–17). From your
knowledge of Louis XIV's reign, what elements of bias can you
discern in Leibnitz' judgements?

5   Remonstrance to Louis XIV, 1694

Sire,

The person who takes the liberty to write you this letter has no
private interests to serve. . . . If he speaks too boldly to you, do not
be surprised, for truth is free and strong. You have hardly ever been
5   used to hearing it. . . .

For thirty years or so, your chief ministers have undermined,
indeed overthrown all the ancient maxims of the state in order to
stretch your authority beyond all limit, an authority which is theirs
since they have been allowed to exercise it. No longer do they speak
10   of the state and its laws; they speak only of the king and his pleasure.
They have increased your revenues and your expenditure to an
enormous degree. They have exalted you to the skies in order to
outshine, so they claim, the grandeur of all your predecessors
combined; in other words, to impoverish the whole of France so as
15   to establish in the court an extravagance, both monstrous and
incurable. They have wished to raise you upon the ruin of the entire
state, as if you could really become great by ruining all your subjects
on whom your true greatness depends. It is true you have been
jealous of authority, perhaps excessively so, but in reality each
20   minister has been complete master within the scope of his
administration. . . . They have been strict, haughty, unjust, violent
and dishonest. They have known no other principle . . . but to
threaten, crush and destroy all those who resisted them. They have
rendered your name odious, and the whole French nation intolerable
25   to all our neighbouring peoples. They have retained none of our

traditional allies. . . . They have caused over twenty years of bloody wars. . . .

Meanwhile, your people, whom you should have loved as your children and who have hitherto been so devoted to you, are dying of
30 hunger. The cultivation of the soil is almost completely abandoned; the cities and the countryside are depopulated; all industry is stagnant: it no longer offers workmen employment. All commerce has been decimated. You have thus consumed half the real wealth and vitality of your kingdom in order to wage war and defend vain
35 conquests abroad. Rather than squeezing money from the poor people, you ought to give them alms and nourish them. The whole of France is little more than a great poorhouse, desolate and with no provisions. . . . The people, who have hitherto had so much confidence in you, are beginning to lose their affection. Your
40 victories and your conquests are no longer a cause of rejoicing; they are full of bitterness and despair. Sedition, so long unknown, is gradually increasing everywhere. . . . Thus, Sire, is the state of things. You live as one whose eyes are fatally blinded.

Fénelon, *Lettre au Roi*, in *Oeuvres de Fénelon*, ed. Aimé-Martin (Paris, 1861), vol iii, pp 425–8

Questions

a What do you understand by 'You have hardly ever been used to hearing' the truth in lines 4–5? Do you consider this a fair comment?

b '[T]he ancient maxims of the state' (line 7). Why does Fénelon believe that Louis XIV's 'chief ministers' had 'undermined, indeed overthrown' these maxims?

c What image does Fénelon create in this extract of (i) Louis XIV (ii) his ministers? From your knowledge of this period, how far and for what reasons are such impressions justifiable?

d 'The whole of France is little more than a great poorhouse' (lines 36–7). What evidence does Fénelon produce in support of this accusation? Compare and contrast Fénelon's description of 'the state of things' in France with that of La Bruyère (Section III, Introduction), and John Locke (Section III, doc. 4).

e Why does Fénelon think that 'the poor people' are worthy of the king's love and attention?

★ f 'Sedition, so long unknown, is gradually increasing everywhere' (lines 41–2). What evidence would you produce to support this claim?

★ g The 'indignation of a public accuser' rather than 'a mere intellectual disagreement' (Hazard). Discuss briefly the significance and importance of such documents as Fénelon's in the light of this quotation. How do they reflect on the 'system created by Louis XIV'?

6   Peace of Ryswick

Greate preparations of fireworks & other pompes for the Kings
returne: Contentions still in Poland twixt Conti, & [Duke of] Savoy:
None got by this peace so much as Spaine who contributed least to it;
the wonder is, why France who had such advantage should yeild to
5   part with such Conquests, & having taken Barcellona which cost
him so many brave men, & was so advantageous an acquist, besides
successe in America; for that it was not want of men nor Mony
appeared by those vast summes sent into Poland; & exceeding rich &
chargeable expense for the Mariage of the D of Burgandy: But 'tis
10   imputed to the decay of his owne health, his apprehension of the
Dolphin, the importunitye of Mad: Maintenon &c: In the mean time
he keeps Strasburg which gives him entrance into Germany, when
he pleases, secures the Swisse to him, having made such Conditions
about Lorrain, as signify little when ever he think fit to breake:
15   Nothing all this while don at all for the poore protestants or their
interests, even in the palatinat it selfe, which shews, how little they
were minded by us or any of the Confederats, since the D. of Sax, &
others go over daily to the Papists, so as the peace is nothing that
which it was hoped.

John Evelyn, 30 October 1697. *Diary*, op cit, p 1018

Questions

a   Identify (i) Conti (line 2); (ii) Duke of Savoy (line 2).

b   What was the Peace of Ryswick?

c   '[T]he Kings returne' (lines 1–2). Where was the king returning
from?

d   Explain and comment briefly on 'Contentions still in Poland'
(line 2) between Conti and the Duke of Savoy.

★   e   Is it true to say that 'None' had gained 'by this peace so much as
Spaine' which 'contributed least to it' (line 3)? How far, do you
think, did the terms of the Peace of Ryswick reflect the true
course of the events of the war?

f   Explain and comment on the historical significance of (i) 'France
who had such advantage' (line 4); (ii) 'having taken Barcellona
. . . an acquist' (lines 5–6); (iii) 'successe in America' (line 7); (iv)
'Nothing all this while . . . hoped' (lines 15–19).

★   g   Identify 'such Conquests' in line 5 and explain why France
decided to 'yeild to part with' them.

h   'But 'tis imputed . . . Maintenon' (lines 9–11). Comment briefly
on each of the three 'causes' which Evelyn attributes to the peace
settlement of Ryswick. From your knowledge of his reign, what
do you consider to have been Louis XIV's real motives behind
the peace settlement?

7 The Spanish Succession

(a) A historian's analysis

The treaty of Ryswick was concluded on at least as fair terms as almost perpetual ill fortune could warrant us to expect. It compelled Louis XIV to recognise the king's title, and thus both humbled the court of St Germains, and put an end for several years to its intrigues.
5 It extinguished, or rather the war itself had extinguished, one of the bold hopes of the French court, the scheme of procuring the election of the dauphin to the Empire. It gave at least a breathing time to Europe, so long as the feeble lamp of Charles II's life should continue to glimmer, during which the fate of his vast succession might
10 possibly be regulated without injury to the liberties of Europe. But to those who looked with the king's eyes on the prospects of the Continent, this pacification could appear nothing less than a preliminary armistice of vigilance and preparation. He knew that the Spanish dominions, or at least as large a portion of them as could be
15 grasped by a powerful arm, had been for more than thirty years the object of Louis XIV. The acquisitions of that monarch at Aix-la-Chapelle and Nimeguen had been comparatively trifling, and seem hardly enough to justify the dread that Europe felt of his aggressions. But in contenting himself for the time with a few strong towns, or a
20 moderate district, he constantly kept in view the weakness of the king of Spain's constitution. The queen's renunciation of her right of succession was invalid in the jurisprudence of his court. . . . By the queen of France's death, her claim upon the inheritance of Spain was devolved upon the dauphin; so that . . . the two great monarchies
25 could be consolidated, and a single will would direct a force much more than equal to all the rest of Europe. If we admit that every little oscillation in the balance of power has sometimes been too minutely regarded by English statesmen, it would be absurd to contend, that such a subversion of it as the union of France and Spain under one
30 head did not most seriously threaten both the independence of England and Holland.

> Henry Hallam, *The Constitutional History of England from the Accession of Henry VII to the Death of George II* (London, Alex. Murray, 1870), p 700

(b) The Young Monarch, Philip V of Spain, to Louis XIV

My resolution has been taken. God has placed the crown of Spain on my head, and I will maintain it as long as a drop of blood flows in my veins. Were I capable of meanly yielding it, you would, I am
35 convinced, disown me for your grandson. Rather let me perish in Spain, fighting the ground foot by foot, than betray the love of my subjects, or tarnish the honour of my House.

> *Mémoires de Noailles* (Paris, 1777), vol iii, letter of 17 April 1708

a Identify (i) 'the king's title' (line 3); (ii) 'the war' (line 5); (iii) Charles II (line 8); (iv) 'The queen' (line 21).

b What reasons does Hallam give here for calling the terms of the treaty of Ryswick 'fair' in line 1?

c Explain and comment briefly on the historical context of (i) 'the scheme of procuring the election of the dauphin to the Empire' (lines 6–7); (ii) 'so long as the feeble lamp of Charles II's life should continue to glimmer' (lines 8–9); (iii) 'The queen's renunciation of her right of succession was invalid in the jurisprudence of his court' (lines 21–2).

★ d 'It compelled Louis XIV to recognise the king's title' (lines 2–3). David Maland calls this condition Louis XIV's 'most difficult obligation'. Comment on this view in an attempt to explain fully Hallam's observation.

e The problem of the Spanish Succession 'was not merely a question of avoiding a union of thrones' (Maland). Discuss this view in the light of extract a.

f Explain fully and comment on the historical context of extract b.

★ g 'My resolution has been taken' (line 32). From your knowledge of this period and in the light of extract b, how realistic, do you think, was Philip V's 'resolution' in 1708? What chances did he have then of '[maintaining] the crown of Spain'?

★ h How favourable were the relevant terms of the treaties of Utrecht and Rastadt to Philip V of Spain?

8   Treaty of Utrecht, 1713

I. That there be a universal perpetual peace and a true and sincere friendship between . . . Princess Anne, queen of Great Britain, and . . . Prince Louis the XIVth, the most Christian king, and their heirs and successors, . . . the kingdoms, states and subjects of both. . . .

5 V. Moreover the most Christian king promises . . . that they will at no time whatever disturb or give any molestation to the queen of Great Britain, her heirs and successors, descended from the . . . Protestant line, who possess the crown of Great Britain and the dominions belonging thereunto. Neither will the . . . most

10 Christian king, or any of his heirs, give at any time any aid, succour, favour or counsel . . . to any person or persons . . . who for any cause or under any pretext whatsoever should hereafter endeavour to oppose the said succession, either by open war or by fomenting seditions and forming conspiracies against such prince or princes

15 who are in possession of the throne of Great Britain. . . .
VI. Whereas the most destructive flame of war, which is to be

extinguished by this peace, arose chiefly from thence, that the
security and liberties of Europe could by no means bear the union of
the kingdoms of France and Spain under one and the same king; and
20 whereas it has at length been brought to pass . . . that this evil should
in all times to come be obviated, by means of renunciations drawn in
the most effectual form, and executed in the most solemn manner
. . . that at no time whatever either the Catholic king himself, or
anyone of his lineage, shall seek to obtain the crown of France or
25 ascend the throne thereof . . . the crowns of France and Spain are so
divided and separated from each other that . . . they can never be
joined in one. . . . Moreover the most Christian king consents . . .
that he will not, for the interest of his subjects, hereafter endeavour
to obtain . . . any other usage of navigation and trade to Spain and
30 the Spanish Indies than what was practised there in the reign of the
late King Charles the Second of Spain, or than what shall . . . be fully
given . . . to other nations and people concerned in trade. . . .
IX. The most Christian king shall take care that all the fortifications
of the city of Dunkirk be razed, that the harbour be filled up, and that
35 the sluices or moles which serve to cleanse the harbour be levelled,
and that at the said king's own expense. . . .
X. The said most Christian king shall restore to the kingdom and
queen of Great Britain . . . the bay and straits of Hudson. . . .
XX. Just and reasonable satisfaction shall be given to all and
40 singular the allies of the queen of Great Britain in those matters
which they have a right to demand from France. . . .
XXX. In witness hereof we the underwritten ambassadors
extraordinary and plenipotentiaries of the queen of Great Britain,
and of the most Christian king, have put our seals to these present
45 instruments, subscribed with our own hands at Utrecht, the 31/11
day of March/April, in the year 1713.
> G. Chalmers, *Collection of Treaties between Great Britain and
> other Powers* (London, 1790), vol i, pp 340–86

Questions

⋆ *a* Why, do you think, was it felt necessary to include clause V in the
Treaty of Utrecht?
   b Comment briefly on the historical context of clause IX.
   c Identify the 'allies of the queen of Great Britain' (line 40). What
'matters', do you think, did 'they have a right to demand from
France' (line 41)? To what extent and in what ways were these
'demands' eventually given 'just and reasonable satisfaction' (line
39)?
⋆ *d* How far did the terms of the Treaty of Utrecht reflect the true
course of the events of the war?
⋆ *e* After Utrecht and Rastadt, Europe was 'neither what [Louis
XIV] had envisaged at the height of his power, nor what he had

been resigned to at his lowest ebb' (Erlanger). From your knowledge of the end of Louis' reign, discuss briefly the validity of this judgement.

9 An Overview of Decline

Louis XIV had formed little by little, without a preconceived plan, a double design which he tried to realise during the course of his reign and which he was forced to abandon . . . only by the course of events. [The first part of his design] was to reduce his subjects to
5 absolute obedience to his commands, and the second part was to reduce Europe to complete submission. . . .

His deliberate designs, especially after 1668, for the submission of Europe to his laws, passed through many stages. At first his designs seemed to work: after Nijmegen the king, installed in the solemn and
10 majestic setting of Versailles, appeared an Olympian god, a *Mars christianissimus* according to Leibniz's expression, or a Jupiter giving orders while holding thunderbolts in his hand. At his command the war in the North stopped and Sweden, vanquished emerged victorious (again at Louis's command) at the treaty of Saint-
15 Germain. Louis XIV is the arbiter of Europe; his armies, his navies, organised by Louvois and Colbert, sustained by the industrial might of the French state, are strong and ready to move, feared by all.

After this apogee of the reign comes the turning point of Louis's career, somewhere between 1682 and 1688. His destiny becomes
20 uncertain. The 'Réunions' in time of peace added to France lands extending up the Moselle to below Trier. The Revocation of the Edict of Nantes further aroused indignation, resolving Europe in its resistance to France. The Truce of Ratisbon in 1684 left Europe in precarious balance. The circle of enemies tightened; and, after the
25 English Revolution, almost all of Europe, with the Maritime Powers leading the way, rose up against the absolutism and the domination of the King of France. Outwardly Louis XIV remained still *le grand Roi*, the great king, invincible; but, in actual fact, things were already changing.
30 The decline of French power begins, slowly, from 1688 to 1697; thereafter it accelerated; this in spite of the radiant moment when Louis XIV told them: 'Messieurs, here is the King of Spain,' pointing to Philip V. However by 1708 the invasion of Flanders took place and in 1709 the king, close to complete humiliation, was saved
35 only by the weariness of the English nation, [shaken] by the political revival and accession of the Tory party to power. Louis XIV is defeated by a coalition, which finds itself divided by a confusion of interests and a diversion of principles that separates the goals of the Maritime Powers from those of the Continent. Already French
40 preponderance is over, at least for the moment; in fact the

dismemberment of the French Empire has begun; its seapower is in decline. The balance of power shifts against France.

> Philippe Sagnac and A. de Saint-Leger, *Louis XIV (1661–1715)* (Paris, Presses Universitaires de France, 1949), pp 647–9, reproduced in translation in *Louis XIV*, ed. John C. Rule (N.J., Prentice-Hall, 1974), pp 129–30

Questions

a Identify (i) 'the war in the North' (lines 12–13); (ii) 'the treaty of Saint-Germain' (lines 14–15); (iii) 'The "Réunions" in time of peace' (line 20); (iv) 'The Truce of Ratisbon' (line 23). ´

★ *b* Is it correct to attribute to Louis XIV the 'double design' mentioned in the first paragraph?

c Comment briefly on the aptness of the imagery referred to in lines 10–12.

★ *d* How valid historically is each of the three reasons given in lines 20–4 as evidence for the uncertainty of Louis XIV's 'destiny' between 1682 and 1688?

★ *e* Is there any contemporary evidence to support the view that 'The decline of French power begins, slowly, from 1688 to 1697' (line 30)? Or are the authors here making use of the privilege of hindsight?

★ *f* How was Louis XIV 'saved' by the 'accession of the Tory party to power' (line 36)?

g Explain and comment briefly on the historical validity of lines 37–9, 'a coalition . . . of the Continent'.

10   The Costs of War

The ultimate objection to Louis XIV's foreign policy is not just that it was immoral, nor that it brought death or misery to millions of people, but that the potential gains were never worth the risks involved, let alone the eventual cost. There is a striking disparity
5 between the enhanced power and organisation of the French state, and the ends to which they were put, a motley combination of dynastic pride, outdated religious antagonisms, and piecemeal frontier annexations. . . . [M]ost of Louis's wars seem almost gratuitous; the partial exception is the War of the Spanish
10 Succession, a conflict which more supple diplomacy should have been able to prevent or limit. The financial consequences for the monarchy were shattering, yet this did not mean that France as a whole was a ruined country at the end of the reign. Great though the hardships had been, recovery was remarkably quick; not even Louis
15 XIV could impose sufferings on his people to compare with those of the 'great winter' of 1708–9, or destroy agricultural wealth on the scale achieved by the great bovine epidemic of 1714. The French

peasantry somehow absorbed the savage blows of royal fiscality and
natural disasters, kept the land under cultivation, and maintained the
20 flow of wealth which supported monarchy and privileged orders
alike. The tax demands of the 1700s may have led to the partial
abandonment of some villages, and to a resurgence of violent
resistance, but they were probably less damaging to the social order
than the expedients used by . . . Pontchartrain in the 1690s. . . .
25 [T]hese . . . along with massive borrowing and periodic
defaulting on interest payments, were still insufficient to cover
military expenditure; the harvest crisis of 1693–4 made the position
dramatically worse, compelling a new initiative. At last the crown
taxed the rich, through the *capitation* tax of 1695. . . . The twenty-
30 odd millions it brought in were far from eliminating the deficit,
however, and the king's pledge to abandon it after the conclusion of
peace meant that it ceased soon after the treaty of Ryswick. The debt
of 1697 remained intact as hostilities resumed in 1701, and the
capitation returned with them. . . .Offices had now become
35 virtually unsaleable, so Pontchartrain's successors Chamillart and
Desmarets had to find other sources of extraordinary revenue. The
issue of paper money resulted in the predictable debacle, while the
intendants were ordered to resume the old practice of imposing
arbitrary *taxes d'office* on the wealthier *roturiers*, always suspected of
40 evading their full obligations. The *gabelle* and other indirect taxes
rose to unprecedented levels, accompanied by a massive increase in
smuggling and other forms of evasion. In 1710, aware that the
capitation had ceased to function properly, Desmarets supplemented
it by the *dixième*. . . . None of this could prevent Louis XIV from
45 dying amidst a virtual state bankruptcy.
Robin Briggs, *Early Modern France 1560–1715* (Oxford,
Oxford University Press, 1977), pp 156–7

Questions

a   Why does the author believe that 'the potential gains' of Louis
    XIV's foreign policy 'were never worth the risks involved, let
    alone the eventual cost' (lines 3–4)?
★ b   For what reasons might a 'more supple diplomacy' have
    prevented or limited the War of the Spanish Succession?
★ c   Who was Pontchartrain and what 'expedients' did he use 'in the
    1690s' (line 24)? In what ways were these 'damaging to the social
    order' (line 23) in France?
d   Explain (i) *capitation* (lines 29, 34, 43); (ii) 'arbitrary *taxes d'office*'
    (line 39); (iii) *gabelle* (line 40); (iv) *dixième* (line 44). The '*intendants*
    were ordered to resume the old practice' (lines 37–8): why had
    this 'practice' been discontinued?

VIII *Deliverance*

Introduction

'[P]eople drank and sang and laughed' (Voltaire), many of them '[pouring] forth insults on seeing the hearse pass by' (Duclos). After an unusually long reign of seventy-two years, Louis XIV breathed his last on 1 September 1715. The destitute people of Paris, acting on the emotional spur of the moment, celebrated their deliverance from the despotic grasp of *le grand monarque*. If their actions were perhaps understandable, were they equally justifiable? The last thirty years or so of the *grand siècle* had erased from living memory the grand moments of triumph abroad and the long span of domestic calm and prosperity and left only indelible scars. 'Abroad the expansionist policy of Louis XIV had suffered severe setbacks. At home the finances were in disorder, the economic position of the country had deteriorated, while the attempt to impose religious uniformity . . . had been a failure' (Lough). If Louis' system and methods of government were necessary, indeed desirable, for France in 1661, were they still so in the last decades of the *grand siècle* for the masses 'who were ground down by poverty, taxation and tyranny'? To what extent was France 'a nation happy in itself and a model to other states'? To what extent was it 'gloomy and downcast'? The glories which were once great seem to have so pathetically passed away.

Ezechiel Spanheim observed that Louis XIV 'had loved glory too much at the expense of his real greatness'. However one looks at Louis in the light of this observation, France should be the one major criterion for assessing the true grandeur of the king. Charles Castel, the Abbé de Saint-Pierre, suggests a working definition of what true greatness is not. 'Great power,' he says, 'when not employed to procure great benefit for mankind in general and subjects and neighbours in particular, will not make a very estimable man. In a word, great power alone will never make a great man.' The concentration of power in the Crown should not be confounded 'with true greatness'.

Although it is generally held that during the post-*réunions* period Louis XIV was no longer the Apollo of the 1660s, it is debatable how much more mature the king had really grown. In 1665 he 'was young and rich,' says Voltaire, 'well served and blindly obeyed, fearing no foreign ruler and eager to distinguish himself by foreign conquests.' Writing over thirty years later, Matthew Prior, 'England's La Fontaine', portrays him as 'an Eastern Monarch with good health for a man of sixty and more vanity than a girl of sixteen.' What, then, was the nature of Louis XIV's 'change'? Was it not more likely that the change in circumstances after 1683–4 moulded in him a different man? The influence of Madame de Maintenon, and perhaps of Père Tellier, his confessor, was being increasingly felt. For, if the Louis of the challenging years of the post-Colbert crisis was as great as the Louis of the sweeping years of military triumph, why was he unable to prevent from crumbling the edifice of a system which he had so manifestly engineered? Now that his team of giants had gone, was his authoritarianism enfeebled as his ambitions and 'former magnificence' were being checked by the rapidly growing weight of international opposition? Was his brand of divinely inspired absolutism gradually succumbing to the greater force of rationalism?

> Even before the end of the reign of Louis XIV [writes M. S. Anderson] political authority and religion had begun to lose their grip; scepticism was increasing, judgements of all kinds were becoming more facile but losing weight and solidity, and individuals were beginning to value their own ideas more than received ones.

The unrest of the time was becoming loud and vociferous. In imperceptible stages France was regaining its 'power to resist'.

One final remark. Louis XIV 'had defects and made grave mistakes,' says Voltaire, 'but if those who condemned him had been in his place would they have equalled his achievements?'

1 Solar Eclipse, 12 May 1706 – Or the blazing sunset?

LOUIS: What shall we do, dear Maintenon? My Grand-Son
 Flies from the Foe, and we are all undon.
 Brabant and Flanders to the Austrian yield,
 So much we suffer'd when we lost the Field;
5 O why am I thus wretched!
MAINTENON: To be plain,
 I'll tell you why, to Flatter you's in vain:
 The fam'd Partition-Treaty was the Cause,
 And England's just resentment, and Nassau's:
10 You own'd a Prince whom they refus'd to own,
 And poor Bavaria's by your Arts undone;
 You trickt the Portuguese.

LOUIS: The Sun, my Dear
    Is now eclips'd and bodes some Ill, I fear.
15 PHILIP [V]: Good Grandsire, take me in again, my Fall
    Is great, and you have been the Cause of all.
    LOUIS: My Love, my Queen, show me what to do?
    For on thy Counsel I depend.
    MAINTENON: Be true,
20 Keep to your Word, forget your usual Fraud,
    For which you're curst at home and loath'd abroad,
    Send the Confederates a Blank.
    LOUIS: 'Tis done;
    What other way was left to save my Crown?

> 'An Appendix containing the Character of the Most
> Christian King, His Virtues and Vices . . .', in *The Life and
> History of Louis XIV present King of France and Navarre*
> (London, John Morphew, 1709), p 41

Questions

a   Explain the historical context of (i) 'My Grand-Son / Flies from
    the Foe' (lines 1–2); (ii) 'Brabant and Flanders to the Austrian
    yield' (line 3); (iii) 'You own'd a Prince whom they refus'd to
    own' (line 10).

b   Comment briefly on the historical validity of lines 8–9. In what
    sense was 'poor Bavaria's . . . undone' by Louis XIV's 'Arts'
    (line 11) and in what way were the Portuguese 'trick't' (line 12)?

★ c   What was the position of Philip V in 1706? How secure, do you
    think, was he then?

★ d   'For on thy Counsel I depend' (line 18). How effective was
    Madame de Maintenon's influence on Louis?

e   'Solar eclipse' or 'the blazing sunset': which do you consider the
    more appropriate to describe Louis XIV in mid-1706? Explain
    why.

2   An Epitaph – a 'devastating testimony of popular feeling'

Louis 14, King of France and Navarre, died on September 1st of this
year, scarcely regretted by his whole kingdom, on account of the
exorbitant sums and heavy taxes he levied on all his subjects. He is
said to have died 1,700,000,000 *livres* in debt. These debts were so
5 great that the Regent has not been able to lift those taxes which the
King promised to remove three months after the peace, the *capitation*
and the *dixième* on all property. It is not permissible to repeat all the
verses, all the songs, or all the unfavourable comments which have
been written or said against his memory. During his life he was so
10 absolute that he passed above all the laws to do his will. The princes

and the nobility were oppressed, the *parlements* had no more power;
it was obligatory to receive and register all edicts, whatever they
were, since the King was so powerful and so absolute. The clergy
were shamefully servile in doing the King's will; he had hardly to
request a grant to be given more than he asked. The clergy has
become horribly indebted; other bodies were not less so. Only the
moneylenders and tax-collectors were at peace, living joyfully with
all the money of the kingdom in their possession.

Written towards the end of 1715 'by a simple parish priest in
the village of Saint-Suplice, near Blois'. Quoted in Briggs, op
cit, pp 164–5

Questions

a   Identify (i) 'the peace' (line 6); (ii) 'other bodies' (line 16).
b   '[H]e passed above all the laws to do his will' (line 10). What
    contemporary evidence would you produce to support this
    claim?
★ c   To what extent and in what ways were 'The princes and the
    nobility . . . oppressed' (lines 10–11) by Louis XIV, since even
    'in the worst moments of financial distress, the French
    government could move only very cautiously in encroaching on
    their exemption from taxation' (Pennington)?
d   Explain and comment briefly on the historical context of lines
    13–16, 'The clergy . . . horribly indebted.'

3   Madame de Maintenon

(a) Madame de Maintenon was a woman of much wit, which the
good company in which she had at first been merely suffered, but in
which she soon shone, had much polished and ornamented with
knowledge of the world, and which gallantry had rendered of the
most agreeable kind. The various positions she held had rendered
her flattering, insinuating, complacent, always seeking to please.
The need she had of intrigues, those she had seen of all kinds, and
been mixed up in for herself and for others, had given her the taste,
the ability, and the habit of them. Incomparable grace, an easy
manner, and yet measured and respectful, which, in consequence of
her long obscurity, had become natural to her, marvelously aided
her talents; with language gentle, exact, well expressed, and
naturally eloquent and brief. . . . She put on . . . an air of
importance, but this gradually gave place to one of devoutness that
she wore admirably. She was not absolutely false by disposition, but
necessity had made her so, and her natural flightiness made her
appear twice as false as she was.

*Memoirs of the Duc de Saint-Simon on the Times of Louis XIV and
the Regency* (Washington, 1901), vol iii, p 11

(b) There was a harmony of mind and manners between [Madame
de Maintenon and Louix XIV] which was destined to increase with
20 age; and her regular, gentle, and serious beauty, heightened by rare
natural dignity, was essentially fitted to please Louis. She loved
consideration as he loved *glory*; like him reserved, circumspect, and yet
full of attraction and grace, she had the same charm of conversation,
and sustained this charm longer by the resources of a richer
25 imagination and a more varied education. Like him she had the
individuality of vigorous and self-seeking organisations, yet she was
capable of lasting and solid, if not ardent, affections. She was at once
less passionate and more constant than the King, who was to be, in
friendship as in love, truly constant to her alone; but she had never
30 known what it was to sacrifice to her feelings either her interests or
her repose; contrary to Louis XIV, she was devoted in small things
and devoid of generosity in great ones. . . .Her calm reflective,
reasoning character, incapable of impulse and of illusion, aided her
to defend a virtue often besieged.

> Henri Martin, *The Age of Louis XIV* (Boston, 1865), vol i,
> p 535

Questions

a   Identify 'the various positions' (line 5) held by Madame de
Maintenon and explain what you think Saint-Simon means by
saying 'She was not absolutely false by disposition, but necessity
made her so' (lines 15–16).
b   List, in your own words, the virtues and flaws which Saint-
Simon sees in Madame de Maintenon. What reservations should
a historian make in using Saint-Simon as historical evidence?
c   What evidence does Martin offer that there was 'a harmony of
mind and manners' (line 18) between Louis XIV and Madame de
Maintenon?
d   'When she attracted the notice of her sovereign she could no
longer boast of youth or beauty' (Macaulay). What then,
according to the two extracts, had Louis, 'the proudest and most
powerful of European kings' (Macaulay), found so attractive in
the bourgeoise woman to choose as his wife?
★ e   'Open [O God, the heart] of the King, that I may set therein the
good that Thou desirest'. Do you consider Madame de
Maintenon's influence on the king to have been entirely one for
the better? Explain fully why.

4   Montesquieu on Louis XIV

(a) Letter XXIV, 1712

The King of France is the most powerful of European potentates. He
has no mines of gold like his neighbour, the King of Spain; but he is

much wealthier than that prince, because his riches are drawn from a
more inexhaustible source, the vanity of his subjects. He has
5 undertaken and carried on great wars, without any other supplies
than those derived from the sale of titles of honour; and it is by a
prodigy of human pride that his troops are paid, his towns fortified
and his fleets equipped.

Then again, the king is a great magician, for his dominion extends
10 to the minds of his subjects; he makes them think what he wishes. If
he has only a million crowns in his exchequer, and has need of two
millions, he has only to persuade them that one crown is worth two,
and they believe it. If he has a costly war on hand, and is short of
money, he simply suggests to his subjects that a piece of paper is coin
15 of the realm, and they are straightaway convinced of it. He has even
succeeded in persuading them that his touch is a sovereign cure for all
sorts of diseases, so great is the power and influence he has over their
minds. . . .

It is said, that, while he was making war against such of his
20 neighbours as had leagued against him, there were in his kingdom an
infinite number of invisible foes surrounding him on all sides. They
add, that, during a thirty years' search, in spite of the indefatigable
exertions of certain dervishes who are in his confidence, not one of
these has ever been discovered. They live with him, in his court and
25 in his capital, among his troops, among his legislators; and yet it is
believed that he will have the mortification of dying without having
discovered them. . . .Beyond a doubt, heaven wishes to punish this
prince for his severity to the vanquished, in afflicting him with
invincible enemies of a spirit and a destiny superior to his own.

(b) Letter XXVII, 1713

30 The King of France is old. We have no examples in our histories of
such a long reign as his. It is said that he possesses in a very high
degree the faculty of making himself obeyed: he governs with equal
ability his family, his court, and his kingdom. . . .

I have studied his character, and I have found certain
35 contradictions which I cannot reconcile. For example, he has a
minister who is only eighteen years old, and a mistress who is
fourscore; he loves his religion, and yet he cannot abide those who
assert that it ought to be strictly observed; although he flies from the
noises of cities, and is inclined to be reticent, from morning till night
40 he is engaged in getting himself talked about; he is fond of trophies
and victories, but he has as great a dread of seeing a good general at
the head of his own troops, as at the head of an army of his
enemies. . . .

He delights to reward those who serve him; but he pays as liberally
45 the assiduous indolence of his courtiers, as the labours in the field of
his captains; . . . he does not believe that the greatness of a monarch

is compatible with restriction in the distribution of favours; and, without examining into the merits of a man, he will heap benefits upon him, believing that his selection makes the recipient worthy.

Montesquieu, *The Persian Letters*, trans. J. Davidson (London, 1891)

Questions

a Why does Montesquieu call Louis XIV 'a great magician' in line 9 and how plausible is his supporting evidence?

b '[H]e has only to persuade them . . . believe it' (lines 12–13). Compare this idea with La Rochefoucauld's in Section VI, doc. 7, *maxime* xiv.

★ c Identify the 'invisible foes' (line 21) and the 'certain dervishes' (line 23) and comment on the validity of Montesquieu's remarks on each.

d 'I have studied his character' (line 34). List, in your own words, what Montesquieu considers to have been irreconcilable 'contradictions' (line 35) in Louis XIV. On the strength of these 'contradictions' and from your historical knowledge, how well, do you think, had Montesquieu come to know Louis XIV?

e Compare and contrast Montesquieu's views on Louis XIV's character with those of Saint-Simon's and Voltaire's in this section.

5   Saint-Simon on the faults of Le Roi Soleil

[T]he mind of Louis XIV was beneath mediocrity, but very capable of improving itself. He loved glory, he wanted order and regularity. He was born prudent, moderate, secretive, master of his emotions and of his tongue, and – will it be believed? – he was also born kind
5   and just. God had given him the makings of a good king, perhaps even of a great king. Evil came to him from the outside. His early youth was so neglected that no one dared to approach his apartment. He was often heard to speak of those years with bitterness. . . . His dependent condition was extreme. He was scarcely taught to read
10 and write; and he remained ever after so ignorant that he never knew the best known facts of history, events, fortunes, careers, rank, or laws. By reason of this deficiency he often fell, and sometimes in public, into the grossest absurdities.

One might have thought that the king would have liked a great
15 nobility . . . far from this; the aversion he felt to nobility of sentiment, and his weakness for his ministers, who hated and kept down, in order to raise themselves, all that they were not and never could be, had given him a like aversion to noble birth. He feared it as much as he feared intellect; and if these two qualifications were
20 united in one person, and he knew it, it was all over with that person.

His ministers, his generals, his mistresses, his courtiers perceived, very soon after he became master, his foible, rather than his real taste, for glory. They vied with each other in praising him, and they spoilt him. Praise, or to speak more truly, flattery pleased him to such a degree that the coarsest was well received, the basest with most relish. . . .

Hence came also the desire for glory . . . hence the facility with which Louvois involved him in great wars . . . hence the ease with which the minister convinced him he was a greater captain than all his generals, both for plans and for execution of campaigns. . . . He believed he was really such as they depicted him. . . .

It is therefore with great reason that one ought to deplore with tears of sorrow, not only an education solely arranged to smother the heart and mind of this prince, and the abominable poison of bare-faced flattery which made a god of him in the bosom of Christianity, but the cruel policy of his ministers who hemmed him in, and, for their own grandeur, power, and fortune, so intoxicated him with ideas of his authority and glory that they corrupted him; and if they did not smother in his soul all the goodness, equity, and desire to know the truth with which God had endowed him, they blunted them and hindered him from making any true use of those virtues, to the lasting injury of himself and his kingdom.

Memoirs of the Duc de Saint-Simon on the Times of Louis XIV and the Regency, trans. K. Prescott Wormeley (Boston, 1899)

Questions

* *a* From your knowledge of the education of kings in the seventeenth century, how fair and valid is Saint-Simon's criticism in lines 6–13?

  b What does the author mean by saying that 'his ministers . . . hated and kept down, in order to raise themselves, all that they were not and never could be' (lines 16–18)? How justified is it to claim that Louis XIV's ministers 'spoilt' (line 24) and 'corrupted' (line 38) him?

  c How does this passage reflect the influence of Saint-Simon's own prejudices? What other sources would you consult to gain a more objective view of *Le Roi Soleil*?

6 Voltaire on the death of Louis XIV

The fortitude with which Louis XIV met his end was unattended by the pomp which had characterised his whole life. His courage even led him to the length of confessing his own faults, and his successor always kept written at the head of his bed the remarkable words

5   which that monarch spoke to him, clasping him in his arms on the
    bed; these words are far other than those commonly reported in all
    the histories, and I give here an exact copy of them:
        'You will soon be the monarch of a great kingdom. What I most
    strongly enjoin upon you is never to forget your obligations to God.
10 Remember that you owe all that you are to Him. Endeavour to
    preserve peace with your neighbours. I have been too fond of war;
    do not imitate me in that, neither in my too great extravagance. Take
    counsel in all things and always seek to know the best and follow it.
    Let your first thoughts be devoted to helping your people, and do
15 what I have had the misfortune not to be able to do myself. . . .'
        This speech is very different from the narrow-mindedness
    attributed to him in certain memoirs. . . .
        Though he has been accused of being narrow-minded, of being
    too harsh in his zeal against Jansenism, too arrogant with foreigners
20 in his triumphs, too weak in his dealings with certain women, and
    too severe in personal matters; of having lightly undertaken wars, of
    burning the Palatinate, and of persecuting the reformers –
    nevertheless, his great qualities and noble deeds when placed in the
    balance eclipse all his faults. Time, which modifies men's opinions,
25 has put the seal upon his reputation, and, in spite of all that has been
    written against him, his name is never uttered without respect, nor
    without recalling to the mind an age which will be forever
    memorable. If we consider this prince in his private life, we observe
    him indeed too full of his own greatness, but affable, allowing his
30 mother no part in the government but performing all the duties of a
    son, and observing all outward appearances of propriety towards his
    wife; a good father, a good master, always dignified in public,
    laborious in his study, punctilious in business matters, just in
    thought, a good speaker, and agreeable though aloof.
        Voltaire, op cit, pp 307–9

Questions

a   Explain the historical context of the first sentence.
b   Louis XIV's 'great qualities and noble deeds when placed in the
    balance eclipse all his faults' (lines 23–4). In what ways does this
    extract bear out this claim?
c   How far does this passage enable you to strike a balance between
    the virtues and the vices that are alleged in documents 4 and 5 to
    have characterised Louis XIV as a king?
★ d 'Time . . . modifies man's opinions' (line 24). Why do historians
    not always share the views of contemporaries? Why are
    historians' interpretations sometimes controversial and their
    evidence conflicting?

7 The limitations of Louis XIV's government

Everywhere, to all outward appearance, the will of the crown was becoming supreme; no class or institution could offer any effective check to its machinery. It was not the overt resistance of any single element that opposed the work of administrative reform, but the
5   inert force of abuses which time had disguised as custom, the 'order' that was the 'disorder of the state'. It should be remembered, too, that the *rationale* of absolutism, the claims that were made for it and the aims that it pursued were more advanced than the machinery for putting it into practice. . . . There is always some margin between
10 theory and practice in the most imposing despotisms of modern times; much less did Louis' government, judged by the tests of its ability to secure uniformity, to enforce law, to raise money as it wished, match the lofty pretensions of Versailles. Words like absolutism or centralisation should not mislead us into thinking that
15 this government was in any sense totalitarian. It was in fact closer to the Middle Ages than to the twentieth century and still at heart *seigneurial*; its view that of the great landowner of a complex estate. The king's own ideal was compounded of rights and duties; for the subject the idea of natural rights had not dawned, he was not yet
20 *citoyen*. To king and subject, the sense of obligation to a natural law was still meaningful. The monarch's estate was fenced with moral limitations derived from this deeply felt superior law – whether it be described as divine or natural is immaterial. In practice, his land was so hedged and ditched with privileges, immunities and enclaves of
25 private right, that he was less a free agent than he seemed. The provincialism of France reflected the manner of her growth over the centuries, by conquest and inheritance. Provinces differed in their weights and measures, their law, their taxation system; they might be divided by internal tolls and customs. Independent enclaves of
30 territory persisted. . . . There were private jurisdictions, even private armies. . . . If with this picture in mind we look back at the lame Leviathan of the seventeenth century, we shall be less surprised to find that it was weak when it came to invading directly the preserves of privilege. . . . The changes in the army and navy
35 amounted to a revolution; justice reached further, and fiscal privilege, hydra-headed, was constantly attacked. The fact remains that the monarchy was never able to break the resistance of the conservative elements that stood in the way of radical reform. . . . [T]he unlimited and stable monarchy of France . . . was not really
40 absolute. It could command the largest army and revenues in Europe, but the limitations were real and thwarting.

> G. R. R. Treasure, *Seventeenth Century France* (London, Rivingtons, 1966), pp 295–7

Questions

★   *a*   What do you understand by 'the inert force of abuses which time had disguised as custom' (lines 4–5)? How and with what success did such a 'force' resist 'the work of administrative reform' (line 4)?

     b   Distinguish between 'absolutism' and 'totalitarianism'. Which of these labels, and for what reasons, would you use to describe Louis XIV's government?

     c   Why does Treasure believe that Louis XIV's government 'was in fact closer to the Middle Ages than to the twentieth century' (lines 15–16)? In what ways was it 'still at heart *seigneurial*' (lines 16–17)?

★   *d*   Is it true that Louis XIV 'was less a free agent than he seemed' (line 25) and that his monarchy 'was not really absolute' (lines 39–40)? Explain fully why.

8   The dark side of the 'grand siècle'

Whereas Richelieu made a brilliant if brutal response to the real problems of his day, Louis XIV . . . remained within the tradition the Cardinal has established. Richelieu's fame is fully justified; enormously intelligent and ruthless, he was the true founder of the
5   absolute monarchy. There is a certain paradox in this, however, for Richelieu himself would surely have been infinitely more flexible and constructive in responding to the new conditions after 1660. Perhaps it was such a feeling which caused Michelet to denounce 'the enormity of the arrogant insanity of Louis XIV'.
10   This comment also reflected its author's concern for the welfare of the people; he was one of the first to recognise the dark side of the *grand siècle*. Quite apart from the devastation war brought to several frontier provinces, the terrible famines came often enough to be part of the experience of most adults. They were dramatic evidence of
15   failures in the finely tuned balance between population and production, whose fluctuations underlay most of the economic difficulties of the period. Smaller variations could already mean starvation for the most vulnerable, unless local charity came to their rescue, while they forced many others to incur crippling debts,
20   tightening the stranglehold of the privileged few over the rural masses. Combined with the efforts of the royal tax-collectors, these pressures helped to turn an ominous situation into a desperate one. . . .
     Strong government and a relatively stable society provided a
25   favourable environment for a higher civilisation, which fed on the great advances in printing, literacy, and education. Here again the benefits were very unevenly spread; the main effect on the mass of the people was to cut them off from the upper levels of French

culture, as their indigenous styles of behaviour and amusement
30   became the object of contempt, even of repression, by the educated
classes. For all the genuine concern of many of its members with the
lot of the poor, the Catholic church came dangerously close to being
another instrument that kept them in their place, while imposing
alien values. The implications of cultural and religious change went
35   far beyond this, of course, and the intellectual developments of the
seventeenth century were in the long run more significant than even
the triumphs of royal absolutism. The kings could tame rebellious
nobles and peasants alike, but they could not destroy the
independent and questioning spirit of writers and thinkers.
40   However confused, impractical, or reactionary the opposition to the
crown still was in 1715, it was a warning sign that autocratic rule
would be tolerated only if it brought material benefits and social
progress. The French monarchy, trapped within the numerous
contradictions of its own nature and history, would find it
45   impossible to satisfy such demands.
Briggs, op cit, pp 208–9, 210–11

Questions

★   *a*   Explain what 'the new conditions after 1660' (line 7) were and
comment briefly on what Briggs considers to be 'a certain
paradox' in the first paragraph.
b   '[T]he enormity of the arrogant insanity of Louis XIV' (lines
8–9). How does the author justify Michelet's denunciation?
★   *c*   How were 'the people . . . cut . . . off from the upper levels of
French culture' (lines 28–9)? In what ways did the Catholic
church come 'dangerously close to being another instrument that
kept them in their place' (lines 32–3)? What 'alien values' (line 34)
did it allegedly impose?
★   *d*   'Because he succeeded in becoming both the sovereign and the
patron of the great men of his age, Louis XIV left an indelible
imprint on civilisation. His was a more difficult and more
glorious masterpiece than a great many conquests' (Erlanger).
Discuss the historical significance and validity of Briggs' last
paragraph in the light of this quotation.